Awesome
Life Tips

365 Tips for Living a Life You Love

By Stephenie Zamora

I dedicate this book to you, my dear reader. May it inspire you to live your best life, love without limits, connect deeply, step into your truth more fully, and guide you towards building the amazing life you're meant to live.

Acknowledgments

....

I would like to acknowledge the following people for assisting me in the creation of this book: Amy Villegas, my phenomenal project manager and right-hand woman, for helping edit the tips in this book, as well as for her direct support in building the Awesome Life Tips following into what it is today; Amy Scott of Nomad Editorial for her pristine editing skills; Meghan Crowley for her assistance and skilled layout of the interior pages; Erika Astrid for creating visual poetry during our photo shoot; Stacie Mahoe for her assistance and support in the early days when I was just beginning to see the potential for my tips; and Jamie DuBose and Marlo Nikkila, my dearest friends, supporters, mentors, and cheerleaders. This book would not be possible without any of you. Thank you so very much.

Introduction

....

There was a time when I truly believed I would never be happy. Throughout my teens and into my mid-twenties, I battled with varying levels of depression and decided I just wasn't wired to be one of those "happy people" who love their lives, feel joyful, and come at each day with a sense of positivity and gratitude. As far as I was concerned, life was always happening to me, and I believed it would always be a struggle. Happiness simply wasn't in the cards for me.

Then one day, working at a job I hated while trying to build my first business, I felt a strong pull to borrow my boss's copy of Jack Canfield's *Success Principles*. Prior to this moment, I'd never read any self-help or personal development books other than those having to do relationships. The very first chapter was about taking 100% responsibility for your life, and it completely changed the trajectory of my life and work.

I began to put the principles of personal responsibility into practice immediately. I'd always been pretty great at taking responsibility for things like not leaving early enough to get somewhere on time or the mistakes I made at jobs and with clients, rather than blaming someone or something else, but with life in general? Not at all. I started to ask myself a very simple question which has become the foundation of my life's work. In every situation that manifested in my life, I would pause and ask, "What did I do to allow this to happen?"

With those nine simple words, I began shifting my perception of everything that was happening in my life. Suddenly, I could see that things weren't happening to me; I was actively creating every situation and experience. This revelation was incredibly liberating because with each answer to the question I gained clarity around how to start making positive changes.

I could see where I neglected to set boundaries in my relationships and how I tolerated (and therefore encouraged) behavior that was out of alignment with my values. I could see where I was attracting negative situation after negative situation and, more importantly, responding as if I were a victim to circumstances rather than the creator of my own reality.

Most important, I realized how my mindset was the key to creating massive shifts in my life without even lifting a finger.

Despite these realizations, creating change wasn't always easy. It took practice, failure, loads of tears, pages and pages of journaling, more practice, and an ongoing dedication to building a life and business I truly loved. The concept of changing our mindset around any given situation is a simple one, but it's far from easy.

The good news is, every single time you step back and ask yourself what you did to allow something to happen so you can evaluate where change is needed, you make a choice. Every single time you pause and take a deep soothing breath instead of stressing out, you make a choice. Every time you choose to respond from a place of positivity, gratitude, trust, and love, you make a choice. And with each choice, you're literally beginning to rewire your brain.

As I write this introduction to my first book of tips for creating a life you love, I can't help but reflect on the journey that brought me here. I so clearly remember the girl I was at the start—lost, frustrated, feeling like a victim, so deeply sad, and lacking fulfillment in all areas of my life.

Today, I live my life from a place of unshakable joy that stems from deep inside my soul. Regardless of what happens in my life, I know that creating a life I love built around my passions is entirely possible for me. It's entirely possible for you, too; you just have to make the choice to take responsibility for becoming the creator that you are. It starts with choosing a new way of showing up in your life and in the world.

I've created this collection of 365 tips to help bring you back to a place of positivity, gratitude, love, and personal responsibility each and every day. It's a practice that requires commitment and devotion, regardless of what comes up or how often you slip up. When you're feeling frustrated, overwhelmed, or like life is happening to you, come back to these pages. Read a tip, close your eyes, take some deep breaths, and then get back out there and start creating the amazing life you're meant to live.

Lots of love,
Stephenie

1

....

Don't wait for a life-changing moment or near-death experience to figure out what's really important to you. Do it right now. What do you really want to do with your life? Who do you want to be and who do you want to be with? Where do you want to live? Be honest about what you want and go for it, starting today. Too late comes far too soon for most people.

2

....

Funky funks, depression, and sad days shouldn't be avoided or rushed through. When you really sit with and experience what you feel, you gain amazing clarity and insight into what you desire and what you need to change. When you avoid feeling it, you miss out on a necessary experience and life lesson. Sadness and hurt hold the keys to happiness and fulfillment. And when it passes, which it always does, you're ready to move forward with clarity and peace.

3

. . . .

Always be yourself. Don't try to sway or stretch your truth in order to win someone's affection or approval. Do you really want to have a relationship with someone who doesn't know, love, and appreciate the real you? The best way to find true connection and deep love is to show up fully as your authentic self. You're perfect, beautiful, and amazing exactly as you are. Let others see that.

4

. . . .

Speak your truth, especially when you believe you're
the only one feeling this way. Your truth may very well
contain the exact words or ideas that help someone else
define what they're experiencing in their own life.
You're never alone in what you're feeling or experiencing
in this world. Instead of suffering in silence, be the voice
that brings people together.

5

....

Say what you want to say to the person you want to hear it. Stop holding back or manipulating the truth of what you think or feel. If you miss someone, say it. If you love them, shout it from the rooftops. If something upsets you, talk about it; you may have misunderstood. Life's too short to miss out on opportunities for real connection, so start speaking up today.

6

. . . .

If you have a goal that's really important to you,
find yourself a coach, trainer, accountability partner,
mastermind, or someone to help you make it happen.
Sure, you can absolutely do this on your own, but
you can also do it a lot faster with the help, guidance,
accountability, and support of someone who's already
done it themselves. Don't be prideful; get support
so you can move forward with ease.

7

....

Make a change today! If you've been wanting to update your wardrobe, switch jobs, move to a new city, or just try a new cereal in the morning, today's as good a day as any to do it. Change is refreshing and necessary for growth. Don't be afraid to switch things up if you feel compelled to do so. There's a reason you're feeling pulled, no matter how big or small the change.

8

....

Remember that everyone's feelings, thoughts, and experiences are 100% valid. You're in no position to say otherwise, or to judge their experience. Just as you're having your own unique experience in this world and in your relationships, they are too. Take the time to listen and understand their point of view. Everyone deserves validation and to be understood and heard.

9

....

Start saying yes at times when you'll typically shy away and say no. Put yourself out there and meet new people, try new things, and have exciting new experiences. Make memories, get out of your comfort zone, and learn something new and different. Always go with your gut, but try to expand yourself and your life once in a while. You never know what it will lead to, and staying comfortable keeps you stuck.

10

. . . .

When you're in a relationship that no longer serves you, the other person won't always make it easy for you to walk away if it affects them and their needs. You have to do what's best for your life and needs. Sometimes you're the only one who supports your changes and choices, but you have to remember you're also the number one person for the job. Follow your heart and do what you need to.

11

....

Learn to manage your own expectations rather than expecting others to. If something isn't laid out clearly for you, don't assume it's going to be the way you want or desire it to be. Ask! Assumptions on your part only lead to completely avoidable disappointments and misunderstandings. Take responsibility and clarify.

12

. . . .

You're never done with personal development, especially when you're working towards making positive shifts in your life. Just because you read or do something that makes you feel a shift doesn't mean you won't still experience down periods. The goal is to keep moving, learning, growing, and shifting. Before you know it, you'll be there, I promise.

13

....

Always turn down the big glamorous clients and opportunities that don't feel right for the deeply fulfilling and better-fitting ones. If your heart's not in it, you're going to do poorly, slip up, or feel miserable and bitter. It's better to politely decline and focus your energy on those people, opportunities, and experiences that nurture your heart and soul.

. . . .

Laugh more. Life is too short to not enjoy it!
Even when times are tough, choose to use joy, humor,
and positivity rather than sinking into despair or
darkness. Make the conscious choice to be a happy
person no matter what's going on. If you're not feeling it,
then just smile. Watch some hilarious online videos
or call a funny friend. Smiling and laughing will
elevate your mood immediately.

15

....

Don't be afraid to be vulnerable with others; it's
the foundation of real, deep connection. If you want
a man who adores and connects with you, a best
friend that knows you inside and out, or a family that
sees and loves you for you, you have to be real, raw,
and vulnerable. It's scary, and sometimes it's really
hard, but it's always worth it. Be brave and get
vulnerable with someone you love today.

. . . .

Learning to speak your truth and be 100% authentic all of the time, around everyone, isn't always easy. In fact, it can feel really hard most of the time. Start small and speak up about the little things like your preference in movies or restaurants. Start a blog and practice sharing your thoughts or feelings. Disagree with the group when you'd normally nod along. The most important thing is to start, even if it's just tiny steps every day.

17

. . . .

Good, kind, and considerate people are all around you.
Just because you have yet to experience them doesn't
mean they don't exist or you're not worthy of having
them in your life. If it sounds too good to be true, maybe
you need to take a good look at the people in your life.
Sometimes we have to let go of the negative people
and beliefs in order for more positive connections
and experiences to come into our lives.

18

....

If someone makes fun of you for something you love,
whether it's a TV show, outfit, hairstyle, or anything else,
just own it! So what if they don't like it? You do,
and that's all that matters. When you own your
preferences and choices regardless of criticism, people
will respect you more. They'll reflect that inner
confidence back to you in the form of acceptance.
Brush criticism off and keep being your awesome self.

19

. . . .

As we have different life experiences and relationships, we change. We learn and grow and shift. There's no point at which this stops; as long as you're alive, change is inevitable. So instead of beating yourself up when something in your life no longer serves you, welcome change with open arms. It's all part of the journey.

20

·················

Instead of going on some crazy diet or exercise plan,
go on the "how does this make me feel?" lifestyle plan.
If you eat something, how does it make you feel?
Does that workout energize or exhaust you?
Does that beverage refresh you or leave you
feeling yucky on the inside? Your body knows
what it needs and communicates it clearly.
You just have to start paying attention.

21

. . . .

Learn how to laugh at yourself rather than taking
things so seriously. At some point in our lives, we've all
tripped, said something ridiculous, made outrageous
errors, or walked around with our fly unzipped.
What's the big deal? Take notice, have a chuckle
with yourself, then move on with your life.
Nothing is as big a deal as you think it is, I promise.

. . . .

Cultivate curiosity about other people, but don't be nosey (there's a big difference). We're all so amazing and different. By using curiosity to learn about others, you're expanding yourself in ways you can't even imagine. Everyone has something to offer, whether it's a life lesson, insight, resource, belief, or a simple laugh. The only way to find these gems is to get curious.

23

. . . .

If life presents you with an opportunity and your intuition says "heck yes!" you'd better listen up and act accordingly. Trying to control every little thing in your life just causes unnecessary stress, frustration, and anxiety. When you loosen your grip, begin listening to and trusting your intuition, and start to enjoy the journey that is life, amazing things happen. You meet the right people, discover the perfect opportunities, grow more quickly, and create what you desire in no time at all.

24

. . . .

Strive to have a full and fulfilling life, not a busy one. The difference is that you're filling your life up with joy, happiness, amazing memories, great people, new experiences, and lots of love and passion. Eliminate things that leave you feeling empty, aren't an equal exchange of energy, or don't add value to your life so you can fill it up with things that do. Having a busy life isn't a badge of honor; it's just exhausting. Having a full life is fulfilling, and worth every moment.

25

. . . .

Don't be spiteful, hateful, or difficult just because
something doesn't go the way you want it to.
And don't hurt someone just because they hurt you.
If it comes as a surprise, take a moment to breathe
before you fly off the handle. Try to see it from the other
person's perspective and realize that, more often than not,
it's not some kind of personal attack on you. Responding
from a negative space only exacerbates the situation,
and that doesn't serve anyone.

....

Learn to roll with life's punches. Be resilient and master
the art of bouncing back. Nothing is ever as horrible
as it seems in the moment, time does heal all wounds,
and you can bounce back stronger than you ever believe
possible. Take a moment to feel what you feel and be
kind to yourself. Allow yourself the time and space to
heal when needed, then dust yourself off and get
back to your life. You can do this.

. . . .

Stop believing you have to explain yourself to everyone or justify your decisions and choices. Are you doing what's best for you? Does it make you feel good/happy/fulfilled? Does it feel like the right timing to you? Awesome, that's all that matters. You're under no obligation to live according to anyone else's feelings, concerns, or opinions about what's best.

28

....

Just because things start to get bumpy or aren't going exactly how you'd like them to doesn't mean that everything's about to fall apart. Whatever journey you're on, there will be obstacles, roadblocks, and times when you question if you're still being supported by the Universe. You always are, and things are always happening as they should. Trust in that and keep moving forward. It's all going to work out perfectly.

29

. . . .

Get your spring cleaning on whenever you feel the urge.
The desire to purge, clear space, or let go of items and
people that no longer serve you is a sign that there are
new and exciting things heading your way. Take the
time necessary to create the space and a clean slate
for awesomeness to manifest in its place.

30

. . . .

Be considerate of others as much as possible,
whether it's other drivers on the road, your family
and friends, or a complete stranger while grocery
shopping. Remember that you're not the only person
that matters. You're part of an amazing community
and world, so be kind, considerate, and respectful
of the people you share this space with.

31

....

Begin looking at your mistakes as opportunities
for growth. What is the gift or lesson in each?
Don't beat yourself up about not being perfect,
or begin to believe the Universe is out to get you.
Focus on what's there to be learned and gained
from this experience. Learn the lesson, then move
forward with your life. There's no point dwelling
on the past and letting it bring your future down.

32

....

Don't put any stress or pressure on yourself to feel
anything other than what you feel right now.
There's nothing wrong with how you feel about whatever
is happening for you right now. Most important, don't
"should" on yourself. Saying things like, "I should be
happy," "I should be more grateful," or "I should be more
put together than this" will only bring you down. Focus
on the present moment, allow yourself the space to feel
your emotions, and move forward when you feel ready.

33

. . . .

Work to release all the baggage you carry from past relationships. That person is gone, so don't blame or punish anyone else for what's left unresolved. Work through it in whatever way you need to in order to heal and release it, then move forward. See people for who they are, not how they compare to someone else, and don't assume they're the same as anyone that's come before them. Holding on to old hurts and resentment is toxic for both you and your new partner. Forgive, release, move forward.

. . . .

If you're feeling stressed out, overwhelmed, vulnerable,
or on edge, take responsibility and do what you need
to do to feel better. Avoid putting yourself in situations
where you end up saying or doing things you'll
later regret. It's a reason and explanation for
acting out, but it's not an excuse and it's not okay.
Just because you have things going on it doesn't give you
permission to unload on anyone else. Take a time-out
and resolve what needs to be resolved.

35

. . . .

You have to learn to love yourself first, before anyone else will be able to love you fully. You set the tone for your relationships as well as the boundaries on how you expect to be treated. Don't put up with disrespectful, hurtful, or inconsiderate people in your life. You deserve better, especially from yourself. When you really love and honor yourself, you'll have zero tolerance for anything but the best from others. Treat yourself like the amazing individual you are, and others will too.

36

....

When someone you love is making poor decisions,
hurting themselves, or making a mess of their life,
you have to remember that it's their life and their choices
to make. The only person causing you grief, anger,
or hurt in this situation is you, by expecting something
different from them or the situation. Choose to love
them as they are, mistakes and all, or remove them
from your life. Don't torture yourself by wishing
it were different or taking responsibility. Just love
them and release your attachment.

37

....

If you're going to waste time procrastinating things
like work or chores, it's better to spend that time doing
something fulfilling and meaningful. Read a good book,
brunch with a friend, work on your craft project, or take
a long walk outside! It's better to make use of the time
than waste it surfing the Web. You'll feel more refreshed
and ready to take on the task at hand, and you'll have
done something worthwhile with the time.

38

. . . .

It's great to have a plan for where you want your future
to go, but learn to live in the moment and let life unfold
as it will. You might meet the love of your life, stumble
into an unexpected opportunity, or find yourself in an
even more amazing spot than you planned for. If you're
saying no because it doesn't fit with the plan you've
created, you could be missing out! Stay focused,
but remain open. Life is full of awesome surprises.

39

....

Everyone in this world experiences fear. Fear of the unknown, failure, success, love, heartbreak... you name it, we've all experienced it. We're all human and fear is a normal and natural emotion. Don't allow yourself to stay stuck because of it. People who are living happy, healthy, and successful lives are those that took action despite the fear. Fear is always going to be there, so learn to feel it and move forward anyway.

40

....

Master the art of making eye contact with others,
whether it's your loved ones, family, friends, or strangers
on the street. Stop hiding your amazing self from the
world behind quick glances in the other direction.
Connect. Smile. Really see the world and the other
amazing people that exist within it. More importantly, let
others see you. No matter how awkward, vulnerable, and
uncomfortable you feel, connection is always worth it.

41

....

Travel as often as you can, even if that just means heading to a random neighborhood you've never experienced in your city, or to a nearby town you've never seen. If you can splurge and go somewhere totally new and different, awesome! But don't let lack of funds keep you where you are. Try to expand yourself as a person by meeting new people, going to new restaurants, and immersing yourself in different cultures and experiences as often as you can.

. . . .

You don't have to always be on. It's okay to dial
it back when your energy's low. Don't exhaust yourself
trying to be a high-energy version of fun, social,
and expressive. You can be all those things at a
lower frequency as well. Show up as you are and at
a level that suits you in the moment. Sometimes
that's dialed back, sometimes that's high energy.
Regardless, you are always the same amazing individual.

43

....

Your way isn't the right way. Just because you follow certain fashion trends, are a certain personality type, or hold certain beliefs doesn't mean the other people in this world are wrong or weird.
We're all different. We're all right in our own ways. Learn to accept and respect those differences. It's what makes the world such a beautiful place and it's how we learn to grow and expand as individuals.

. . . .

If something doesn't work for you, it doesn't work for you, and that's okay. You don't have to explain yourself or defend your decisions to anyone else. If it's not a good fit, it's not a good fit, end of discussion. You have the right to make decisions in your best interests based on what you feel is right or not. Trust and honor yourself. Don't defend and explain; knowing what feels right or wrong is enough.

45

....

It's not your responsibility to care about or solve every problem in this world. You were put here with specific skills, passions, and interests, so focus on what speaks to you, tugs at your heart, and matters most to you. There's someone else out there concerned with the things you aren't, so don't worry that you're not doing enough around something you don't truly care about. You have your place in this world, the same as everyone else.

....

Be compassionate. It's impossible to fear or hate anyone or anything you truly understand, so seek to understand. Work to understand others' point of view and why they are the way they are, then practice compassion. You have no idea what it's like to be in their shoes, so show love rather than fear, kindness rather than cruelty, and acceptance rather than judgment.

47

....

If you're working towards a goal and you can't seem to make it happen, it might be time to find a new kind of motivation. Sure, you may want to create something at a surface level, like buying a new car or getting in awesome shape. But what core feelings or experiences do you really want to have? Dig deep into the why behind your current goal and see what gems you can uncover that will help you get there faster.

48

....

It doesn't make you important, successful, or special to be stressed out all the time. It just means you're stressed out all the time! Stop believing anxiety, overwhelm, and stress are badges of honor just because that's what society rewards. We're not actually impressed that you're stressed. Instead of constantly complaining, find ways to shift to calm, relaxed, and joyful. Do things that light you up. Relax a little. You'll accomplish far more this way.

49

....

Don't be upset when people you love aren't excited
as you take steps to follow your dreams, especially
when it involves risk of any kind. Remember that they
love and care for you and may show concern, but also
that you may be operating outside their level of comfort.
Their negativity or fear has nothing to do with you
and your abilities! Try not to allow other people's fears
and discomfort to derail you. Focus on what you
want, and trust that you'll get there.

50

....

Get started on your big dreams and goals today.
Regardless of how big and unreachable they may
seem to you right now, there's always something you
can do today to start making progress. Work backwards
from the big end goal and create mini milestones and
micro-goals until you identify something specific that
you can do right now, and then go do it! Anytime you
feel overwhelmed by something on your to-do list,
just break it down into something easy to take action
on in the moment. You'll get there.

51

....

When you allow yourself to feel what you feel,
you give yourself permission to say that something isn't
right. You'll be able to say that something has to change,
you deserve more or better, or you desire something
new and different. When you give yourself permission
to speak your truth, you take the first step towards
making positive shifts. In order to speak that truth,
you have to start by acknowledging the truth of
your feelings and present experience.

52

Don't let someone else's struggle determine whether you try something. That was their experience, and it in no way determines whether you'll fail or succeed. You're a different, unique person living your own life. Take the risks that feel right and try the things you want to do. Heed their warnings when it resonates with you, but follow your intuition. You always know what's best for you. Don't let someone else's failure or fears hold you back.

53

....

Let failure and mistakes be your teachers. There is always a lesson to be learned, so stay positive and seek it out. Where can you improve? What can you do differently going forward? How is this going to help you become a better, happier, and healthier person? What changes should you make? Find the lesson and move forward.

54

....

You don't have to do things just because your family and friends really want you to. Yes, it may be something that's important to them, but what about what's important to you? What about what you want and need? You get to decide whether it's more important to you to honor your needs or to honor the needs of those around you.

55

....

Surround yourself with people that push you to be better, stronger, and more authentic, and who help you grow as an individual. If you can't find that in family and friends, then find a coach, trainer, or other professional to help you. Don't stay stuck where you are forever just because the people around you have chosen that for themselves.

. . . .

In order to become the person you're meant to be, living the amazing life you're meant to live, sometimes you have to go through hard times. Sometimes you have to be broken down so that you can learn, grow, release, and recalibrate. When times are tough, remind yourself that what is happening to you is happening for a reason.

57

....

Pick one thing that you've always wanted to do and do it, no matter how random or silly it may seem. Sign up for salsa lessons, take up a new sport, or buy supplies for that craft project. The only way to grow as a person and have a life you love is to start following your whims and doing things simply because you want to.

. . . .

Don't be afraid to release people and relationships from your life. The person you want to become and the life you want to live requires that you move forward, grow, and experience certain things. Stop letting someone who doesn't serve you keep you stuck. If it's not right, release yourself from the situation.

59

....

If you're going to self-medicate when you're feeling stressed, depressed, angry, or any other emotion, do it with something healthy. Write and process your feelings in a journal, schedule a smoothie date with your best friend, find a cardio workout you enjoy, or start a meditation practice. Do something healthy and healing.

60

....

Everything is negotiable. You have the right to stand
up and say, "This doesn't work for me, but here's what
I want instead." If you want to make changes in your
relationship, job, financial situation, or anything else, you
have to be clear on what you want and ask for it. Even if
the answer is no, at least you know and can move on to
find something that works better. You deserve to
be happy and comfortable in every situation.

61

....

It's not your responsibility to help someone you love make positive shifts in their life; it's theirs. All you can do is show up to love and support them. Offer them insights and feedback when they ask, but leave the action in their hands. Outside of that, focus on living your best life and know that they'll make the shifts they need to make when the time is right for them.

62

....

There isn't a person out there who can do it all.
It's okay to admit when you're feeling overwhelmed
or when you simply don't have the capacity to get
everything done that needs to be done. Ask for help,
hire it out, or change your plans to better suit where
you're at. There's power in recognizing and admitting
you need help; it's not failure or defeat.

. . . .

Sometimes when you shift gears and start moving in a new direction, it feels like the Universe is no longer supporting you because there's a lull. Oftentimes, the Universe is simply rerouting, recalibrating, and making some shifts in order to bring you the support you need. Be patient and trust yourself and your intuition. Support will always follow, even if it doesn't seem to be the case right away.

64

....

Take a moment to determine if what you're craving in your life right now is a true desire, a calling from within or an intuitive knowing of what you need, or if you're "shoulding" on yourself. Don't do something just because you think you should; do it because you know and feel in your body that you need it. When we follow our desires over shoulds, we create amazing things.

65

. . . .

Stop playing it safe when it comes to connecting with others and expressing yourself. Be open, honest, and upfront about your needs, feelings, experience, or opinions. You will likely alienate someone in the process, but that's the point. By eliminating the people who don't respect your views or belong in your life, you make room for those that do.

66

....

If you don't feel, you won't heal. Rather than stuffing down your emotions, allow them to surface, no matter how heavy they may be. Process them however you need to, take time to treat yourself well, and allow it to pass. If you stuff it down inside, it will resurface later as something far worse, like depression or even illness. It's so much better and healthier to feel and release it as soon as possible. You'll be happier and more at peace as a result.

67

....

Live life with a sense of urgency, because even if
you get to live a long one, it's still incredibly short.
Don't save things for a special occasion; go out and do
the things you want to do, tell people how you really feel,
and stop wasting time and energy on things that really
don't matter. You don't have all the time in the world,
so make the most of this moment.

68

....

There's no right way to do things, because we're all different. Be clear with others about your personal preferences, boundaries, and working style. Let them know the best way to communicate with you and find out the best way to communicate with others. The sooner we all become aware of our unique preferences, the happier we'll all be.

69

. . . .

Don't do something for someone unless you want
to, and don't do it expecting something in return.
Just because you do something for someone doesn't
mean they owe you something, unless you've specifically
discussed that kind of give and take. Do things because
you want to help or support someone, not so people owe
you. Being of service is far more fulfilling than being
someone who everyone owes something to.

70

....

Pay attention to the words you use when you talk.
Instead of hate, can you say, "I strongly dislike"?
Instead of can't, can you say, "I presently struggle with"?
Our words have energy attached to them,
actual vibrations that affect both ourselves and
those around us. Choose your words wisely
and make small shifts where you can.

. . . .

Try not to automatically go on the defense when someone gets upset with you. Take a moment and breathe. Really listen to what they have to say and what they're feeling. They have just as much right to feel upset as you do to feel frustrated by the situation. Try to be compassionate and understanding and keep the lines of communication open. When we respond with openness, it allows space for healing and connection.

. . . .

Oftentimes, blocks come from not realizing we're being given exactly what we asked for, in exactly the way we need it. You might not be the person you need to be in order to really thrive in that job, relationship, or experience without going through something else first. So when the Universe delivers something that seems random, trust that it's what you need first, before you can receive what you asked for.

73

....

Approach every task, situation, and opportunity with a possibility-focused mindset. Instead of thinking about how hard or impossible something may seem, focus on the possibility of what could happen. You're stronger, smarter, and more capable than you give yourself credit for. When you open up to possibility, you'll see just how much you can handle, and it's usually far beyond what you thought you could do.

74

....

Pay attention to whether you're sending out love because you felt the urge to express it, or because you were seeking it in return. If you're seeking it in return, it's going to feel off to the other person. Ask yourself how you can generate that same feeling on your own, for yourself. Stop depending on other people to feel love.

75

....

Your intuition is always speaking to you, but if you
can't hear it, you're going to miss the signs that tell
you whether something is or isn't right for you.
If an opportunity, relationship, or next step is right
and in line with the natural flow of things, your intuition
will know, even if the rest of you is completely freaked
out by the idea. Create the space to listen and
learn to trust what you hear.

. . . .

Stop taking your health for granted; it's not a given,
and everything you do has an impact on it. Where can
you make improvements in your routine or habits?
Maybe it's just starting to take a multivitamin every
day, actually using that gym membership, or switching
from fruit to green juice. Every little bit counts, so start
making small, manageable shifts in a healthier direction.
You'll thank yourself for it in the long run.

. . . .

Never knock something you haven't experienced firsthand. Whether it's a belief, book, product, service, or person, stay open to experiencing and trying new things without taking on the judgments of others. Don't write it off based on someone else's opinion, society's rules, or anything other than your own intuitive hit and personal experience.

....

Do what you say you're going to do. If you're
not sure you can, say so, and don't make promises
that you can't deliver on. Be a person of your word
and be honest if something won't work for you.
Equally as important, if something changes,
communicate those changes immediately; don't just
leave someone hanging or wondering.

. . . .

Make "brain dumps" a regular practice in your life.
Write down absolutely everything that you need or
want to do: errands, tasks, emails, phone calls, ideas,
projects, etc. Anything floating around in your head,
get it down on paper. Then go through and create
priorities from there. You'll be able to move forward
with focus and ease, and you'll have everything
captured in one space so you don't forget.

80

....

Sometimes changes don't make sense or don't look exactly how we'd like them to, but that doesn't mean it's not what's supposed to happen next for us. Opportunity and growth don't wait around until you're ready or it fits with your current life plan. It happens when it's supposed to happen. Don't block the flow by clinging to your plan. Be open and allow things to unfold naturally.

81

. . . .

Take time to celebrate things in your life: the new job,
the anniversaries, the small wins, and the opportunities.
Life is as special as we make it, so choose to make
everything count. You don't have to drop a ton of money
or do anything extravagant; just go the extra mile and
do something out of the ordinary. Your life and
everything in it is worth honoring.

....

Sometimes we have to step away from the people
and things in our lives in order to check in with
ourselves to see what we really need. It can be hard
to hear the tiny whispers and intuitive inner voice
when we're distracted by the day-to-day interactions,
stresses, errands, and to dos. Whether it's
an afternoon or a whole week on your own,
give yourself and others permission to take that space.

83

....

Work to cultivate a spiritual practice for yourself. It can be as simple as connecting to your intuition and body through silencing the outside world. Meditate, pray, go for walks in nature, or simply take the time to breathe deeply with your eyes closed. Allow yourself the space to hear your intuition and connect with your own soul.

84

....

Some things are out of your control, and that's okay.
Take a deep breath and let the situation be what it is.
Try not to stress yourself out further by wishing/hoping/
wanting something different. Ask the Universe for what
you want, release it or take action where you can,
and be open to whatever solution comes. Trust.
The Universe is supporting you.

85

. . . .

If you spend most of your time reminiscing about the good ol' days of college or high school, then it's time to build a life of fun, pleasure, growth, and passion right now. Stop living in the past and start creating a life you're over-the-moon happy to be present in. You can create a bucket list, start traveling, take a class, and try new things whenever possible. The best time of your life can be right now, as long as you take the time to make it so.

....

If you're spending long periods of time feeling off or like
something's on your mind, but you're not sure what,
then you're likely out of sync with your intuition.
When you're in sync, you immediately know what needs
to change, what's right or wrong for you, and what's next.
Make reconnecting with your intuition a priority,
and things will begin to fall into place.

87

. . . .

Don't expect people to know exactly what you know
about any given subject, and don't ridicule them when
they don't. We're all unique individuals with completely
different backgrounds, cultures, education levels,
life experience, and personalities. Remember, you don't
know everything either, and there's always something
new you can learn from others.

....

You have to get uncomfortable to take yourself and your life to the next level. It's all about stretching, growing, changing, and stepping up to a whole new playing field. It's not always going to be easy and you have to understand that. If you can't get uncomfortable, you're going to block the flow and stay stuck exactly where you are. Just lean into the discomfort a little further every day, and you'll get there.

....

If the chores are piling up, your to-do list is mounting, and work is ridiculously busy, take a break. Go for a walk, work out, check in to a spa for a massage, or do what you need to do to give yourself and your brain the space to rest and rejuvenate. Problems will seem smaller, ideas and answers will come to you quicker, and you'll be far more productive when you return.

90

....

Don't assume the worst. When you find yourself doing so, ask yourself if you know your assumption is absolutely true. The answer is always going to be no when it comes to things other people say and do. You don't know what's driving them or going through their head or what their intentions were, so ask, don't assume.

91

....

When you find yourself telling a story about your current situation (expertise, weight, relationship, abilities, etc.), stop and take a deep breath. Get out of your head and reengage in the present moment. Once you're back, shift your story to something positive and true. You are making progress, learning, and growing, and you are also amazing and worthy.

92

....

You can be grateful for what you have in your life
right now and also make moves to change things
up completely. Don't settle for less than you desire or
deserve just because you have more than someone else.
Appreciate what you have and be grateful for your
present circumstances, but don't feel like you can't
also desire something different. Go after what
you want; you deserve it.

93

....

What bad habit causes the most stress in your life?
Is it running late, poor financial management, or eating
foods that leave you feeling sluggish? Find one little way
you can take a baby step towards altering this habit.
Nothing major, just a small tweak you can make every
day. Commit to this new tweak for 30 days, then find
another small step you can take. Repeat, repeat, repeat
until you've shifted this habit for the better.

94

....

It's okay to feel bad, as long as you allow that feeling to be what it is without making it into anything more. It's a matter of saying to yourself, "In this moment, I feel bad, and that's okay." Don't tell yourself a story about why you feel this way or make yourself feel worse. Take a nap, eat a piece of dark chocolate, or call a friend. Do what you need to do to feel better, but don't let your mind turn it into anything more than what it is.

....

Stop ignoring what needs attention in your life.
Face your debt or pile of bills and create a budget.
Talk to your significant other about the issues in your
relationship. Ask for a raise or a better working situation.
Return the dreaded phone call. When you deal with
your issues, you can move forward and create space
for better, more amazing things to happen.

. . . .

Don't be afraid to negotiate the terms of anything in
your life. Do you want to spend less on something?
Do you need more time? Do you want a flexible schedule
or maybe some additional benefits? Higher pay?
All you have to do is ask. If they say no, they say no.
But you also open up the possibility of them saying
yes and creating something you're happier with!

. . . .

Your worth as a person isn't defined by what you have,
the title you hold, the amount of money in your bank
account, or how many people like you. You're already
worthy of infinite love and divine support.
Stop seeking validation, acceptance, and love
outside of yourself; everything you need to feel
whole and complete lies within.

....

Don't allow yourself to freak out over the future. Instead, bring yourself back to the present moment. In this very moment, you're just fine and everything's okay. Start from the space of knowing this and work to create a future that continues to support you. What can you do right now to ensure that down the road, you're just as okay as in this moment? What can you do in this moment to bring joy, fulfillment, and connection into your life? Go do that instead of worrying about the future.

99

. . . .

Only focus on two to three areas of your life that you want to make shifts in at any given time. No more than three and less is even better. Dedicate yourself to the goals in those areas and let everything else fall to the side for now. When things, invitations, or tasks come up, ask yourself, "Is this contributing to or taking away from [Life Area/Goal]?" Act accordingly. The only way to make significant progress with what you want to create is to focus your time and attention on the priorities.

100

....

Don't be afraid to say what you want to say. Wouldn't you rather know how someone feels, be able to say you tried, or have the opportunity to experience something deep and meaningful than to spend the rest of your life wondering what could have been? Far too often we let fear get the best of us when we have the opportunity to create something amazing with someone we care for. And if it doesn't work out, at least you tried.

101

....

Take some time for yourself. Even extroverts who love
and adore everyone around them need space to grow into
the people they're meant to be. That simply can't happen
if you're never alone, so create the space to reconnect
to yourself, explore your desires, think, and just be.
Everyone will still be there when you're done, and you'll
have even more to contribute to the conversation.

. . . .

Only give to and support people because you want to.
Don't do it expecting anything in return. Not only
will this help you lead a more fulfilling life, but you
won't be let down or disappointed, nor will you ruin
relationships over resentment and expectations.
Give when you want to give, love when it's needed,
and set boundaries with those who take advantage.

103

....

Start making healthier choices in your life, whether that means swapping out white rice for brown or taking the stairs instead of the elevator at work. Small changes add up in a big way. Starting small also helps you transition into a new mindset and way of living with grace and ease, ensuring that the changes stick!

....

No one becomes a great success without a tribe, team,
or support group. As you begin working towards your
dreams, the people that don't belong in your life,
don't lift you up, or hate on you for your success,
will begin to fall away. While it can be isolating at first,
remember it's opening up space for the right,
more supportive and uplifting people to step in.

105

....

Get off the free train in life. If you don't invest
in yourself and your goals, you're never going to
experience the changes you desire. Start investing,
even if you start small. You're more likely to do the
work, show up, get honest, and stay committed if you've
actually invested (financially or through any other
form of energetic investment). You're worth it and
you deserve the best in life.

. . . .

Remember, not everyone around you can see the
possibilities you're capable of seeing for yourself.
Don't let outside beliefs (or lack thereof) limit what
you work towards creating in your life. Hold true to
your vision no matter what other people say or believe.
You wouldn't have this particular dream or goal
if it wasn't possible for you to achieve. Trust that
and keep moving forward.

107

....

Just because you don't understand, desire, or feel
something doesn't mean it's not possible for someone else
to. If you don't understand what someone is experiencing,
then the best thing you can do is simply love and support
them. Don't allow your lack of understanding to turn it
into anything other than what it is for them. Let them be
and allow them to feel what they feel. You don't have to
understand to be supportive. You just have to be there.

108

....

Never be ashamed, embarrassed, or regretful of your past. We've all made mistakes, dumb decisions, or bad moves. We're human and it happens to the best of us. Everything you've done and experienced has shaped the amazing person you are today and the wonderful life you're going to live. Make peace with your past and own it. When you own it, it can't own you, bring you down, or come back around to bite you in the butt. It's part of who you are, so work to look at it with love and acceptance.

109

....

Not everyone is going to understand your dreams, callings, and desires all the time, especially your family and friends. They love you and want the best for you, but their desires and expectations cloud their ability to fully see and support what you want to bring to life for yourself. Don't be discouraged and try to see it as an act of love. Then, find a tribe of like-minded people who know how to support you and keep moving forward.

110

....

It's okay to admit that something's not your strength. This isn't about being negative; it's about being honest about where you excel and where you don't. If there's something you're not good at and you simply don't want to learn to be better, find a way to get the support you need so that things continue to run smoothly.

111

....

It's okay to want to change yourself, your body, or your life, so long as you first work to completely love yourself, your body, and your life as they are now. Being grateful, kind, and gentle with yourself is essential to making those shifts you desire. You have to love and support yourself as is before you can create something new.

112

....

Never let someone make you feel bad about who you are, what you do, or the things that make you unique. Whether or not you feel bad about something that's said is 100% up to you. Choose to stand proud in who you are and own whatever decisions, style, preferences, habits, or opinions you have. You always have a choice, so choose to focus on what matters to you, not other people's opinions and judgments.

113

....

If the best time of your life isn't right now, then you
may need to make some changes. Ask yourself,
"What would it take for me to feel 100% happy with
my life (or an area of my life) right now? What would I
need to stop doing?" Then, start taking tiny steps towards
creating a shift or completely overhauling. You deserve an
amazing life in this moment. Not someday, today.
What will you do to start?

114

....

Sometimes you just need to be alone, and that's okay. It doesn't mean anything's wrong with you, or even that anything's wrong in your life. Sometimes you need to create the space to soul search, recover, think, rest, and just be. You don't have to apologize for needing or taking this space, especially if it's part of what makes you a happy, healthy person. More often than not, the things that seem selfish are the things that allow us to show up better for others. So take the space you need.

115

. . . .

Just because you like doing something one way doesn't mean everyone else feels the same, or that you have a right to criticize them for how they choose to do it. Before you open up your mouth about how something's being done, consider that your way might be wrong in their eyes. Be respectful and start by asking why they're doing it the way they are; you may just learn something new. And remember, to each their own, yourself included.

116

....

Take time each day to work on a personal project or goal for your own happiness and well-being. Even if it's only ten minutes a day, start making progress on something that lights you up. Paint, write, craft, bake, plot, and make connections. Do something. Even on the worst of days, this little act will make a world of difference. You'll feel more productive and fulfilled, and like you're making progress, because you are.

117

. . . .

If you're in a toxic or unhealthy relationship, remember that while it's never okay for someone to treat someone else poorly, you chose (and continue to choose) to be in that relationship. You're also choosing, right now, whether to set boundaries, say enough's enough, or walk away. Take responsibility for the situation and start making choices that truly serve you.

....

Go on a no-stress or low-stress diet. You can begin to crowd out stressful people, experiences, and things by adding ones that relax, rejuvenate, and energize you, such as new friends, meditation, candlelight baths, and trips to the beach. Start making better choices and soon it will be easy to release those things that really stress you out.

119

. . . .

When you experience fear around pursuing your
dreams, ask yourself, "What's the worst that could
happen?" Ask yourself that question repeatedly until
you're at the very final end result of "the worst."
Compare that to the idea of allowing your life to
pass by without ever giving your dream a shot,
and you'll see that the worst probably isn't that bad
compared to living a passionless, unfulfilled life.

120

....

Don't try to change your whole life at once;
you'll just overwhelm yourself. Instead, focus on a
few things that are really important to you right now.
The more focused you are, the faster you'll accomplish
any changes or goals you wish to. Be adamant that any
activity, experience, or interaction that doesn't directly
move you forward in your priority areas is not a focus
for you at this time. You can revisit them later, or make
exceptions as you feel compelled to, but stay focused
on what you're working to create right now.

121

....

You're not your failures, just the same as you're not your successes. You're just you, in all your awesome and unique glory. Don't define yourself by anything external you've done, the titles you hold, the mistakes you've made, or the things that you own. You're enough as you are and you're worthy of love and success without any of those things. Just be here in the now and allow yourself to move forward without the baggage of the past.

122

....

Choose to perpetuate love and light in the world, rather than fear and darkness. Instead of sharing awful or tragic news, share something that moves people to joyful tears, is spiritually nourishing, or further proves that people and the world are actually very good and loving. You are responsible for the energy you bring to the conversation; work to make it positive so that we can all be uplifted and inspired.

123

....

With every income bracket, new level of depth or connection in your relationships, and every big step you take towards your dreams and goals, new stuff is going to come up — limiting beliefs, blocks, issues, and mindsets that don't serve you. The question becomes, how bad do you want what you want? Becoming the person you're meant to be means working through a lot of stuff, and not just once! What will you do to remove the blocks?

124

....

Your body is strong and capable, but make sure you
listen to it when it's hurting or unhappy. You only get
one body, so it's your responsibility to care for it as
well as you can. Eat foods that nourish you, drink lots
of water, move your body, and rest when you need to.
Your body will serve you well for years to come
if you take good care of it now.

125

....

When you're working on projects or goals that light you up (aka your passions), you have more focus, energy, and stamina. You need less sleep, comfort food, and negative fixes throughout your days. Passion is the cure for all that ails you, and it will transform your life. Make it a priority to figure out what truly, deeply lights you up, and do those things as much as possible.

126

Go outside, take your shoes off, and stick your feet in the grass, dirt, or sand. Reconnect with nature, breathe in the fresh air, and soak in the sunshine. Be still, listen to the sounds, and just breathe. We live such technology-driven lives, so it's important to take a time-out every now and then to be in nature. Leave your smartphone inside and take in the world around you.

. . . .

Don't waste time on people who won't make time for
you. You deserve to have people in your life who love,
support, and care for you, and not just when they need
something in return. Remember, you're an amazing
individual and it's a privilege for someone to be in your
life and hold space for you. Choose wisely and
release the people who no longer serve you.

....

If you want to become an action taker, you have to know what actions you'd like to be taking. Sit down and make two lists. On list A, write out the things that bring you joy and pleasure and increase your well-being. On list B, write out the action items or things you need/want to do to move forward towards your goals. When you find yourself with extra time, look at your lists and choose to take action on one item. If you're in a productive mood, choose from list B. If you need some fun, some downtime, or to relax, choose from list A.

129

....

Stop apologizing all the time. If you're in the habit of saying sorry to everyone for everything, knock it off. Learn to own who you are and say what you mean. Don't be cruel or hurtful on purpose, but stop apologizing for who and how you are. Feel your feelings freely, say what you're thinking, and be true to yourself. It's also not your responsibility to apologize when someone else is hurting or having a rough day. Practice giving love rather than apologizing for something that has nothing to do with you.

130

....

Choose to make the most of each moment
you have with the people you love. Don't be afraid
to love deeply, express yourself, or ask for what
you need. Our time is short and precious, and you
don't always get a second chance. If you love someone,
tell them. If you miss someone, call. Do what you
need to do before it's too late.

131

....

Do little things that make you happy every single day. This might mean lighting a scented candle, going for a walk to watch the sunset, or using your favorite dishes for dinner. Dress up, play music, and have yourself a dance party. Little infusions of joy will dramatically change your state of mind and, ultimately, your life.

132

....

You're human and therefore you make mistakes. You may have hurt someone, messed up big time at work, or made a huge financial error. What's done is done, so don't allow it to define you for the rest of your life. The person you were and the mistakes you've made mean nothing. What matters is how you show up and what you do today.

133

. . . .

Saying no doesn't mean you don't love or support someone. It means you understand that in order to best love and support them, you can't overextend yourself. If you can't or don't want to do something, say no with love. "Thank you, but no" goes a long way. Honor yourself and your relationships by giving the gift of no.

134

....

Learn how to laugh at yourself! Life is supposed to be joyful and fun, so stop taking yourself and everything else so seriously. Everyone messes up, trips, says the wrong thing, and makes a fool of themselves from time to time; it means you're human like the rest of us. Instead of bumming out, have yourself a laugh and move on! Life will be more fun, enjoyable, and fulfilling if you do.

135

. . . .

Take a Self-Care Time-out at least once every day.
Whether it's 15 minutes in the morning to meditate,
a quick jaunt to the local park at lunch for some fresh
air, or painting your nails and listening to your favorite
tunes, make this time-out a regular practice. Do things
that rejuvenate your soul and make you feel good.
It's about self-care, not productivity.

136

....

Don't pursue something just because you're good at it.
If you don't truly love it, you'll get stuck venturing
down a path or into a career that will only leave you
feeling empty and unfulfilled. The things you're good
at are often skills and talents that were given to you to
support your passions and purpose in this world.
Find a way to merge the two instead of settling
for something that doesn't light you up.

137

....

Stop simply accruing ideas for how you can take action or change your life and start going out and actually doing the work. You can vision board, plan, scheme, and dream all you want, but until you start taking regular, inspired action, the Universe won't respond. It's not a genie in a bottle; it meets you halfway. What's something you can do today to start moving forward?

138

....

What are you avoiding? Sit down right now and
deal with one task you've been putting off. It may be
responding to an email, calling a client you don't want to
deal with, or looking at your bank account. Avoiding the
task only amplifies the energy drain. Dealing with it will
make you feel so much better, even if it's stressful.

139

....

Do one thing every day that scares you or pushes you to grow as a person. Get uncomfortable, stretch yourself, or learn something new. Life's too short not to take risks, put yourself out there, or learn what you're capable of. You're capable of amazing things. Isn't it time you discovered exactly what those things are?

140

. . . .

Give credit and appreciation where it's due. Thank and give credit and appreciation to the teachers, mentors, resources, and amazing individuals that supported you in becoming the person you are today. Everyone appreciates being appreciated, so spread the love and thanks. It doesn't make you any less amazing or capable to acknowledge who and what helped you get here.

141

. . . .

You're worthy of whatever you desire and for no other reason than the fact that you're alive. You're worthy of love, success, support, health, and happiness. Stop holding back or limiting yourself because you believe you're unworthy. Regardless of what's happened in your past, or what others have told you, it's not true. You're worthy. You deserve the best. Ask for what you want and take action towards creating it for yourself.

142

....

It's very rare to find a deep connection with another human, whether that's a friend or a lover. When you do, and it brings you tremendous joy, make the time and give the effort necessary to sustain it. Show your love and appreciation. Continue to deepen the connection. Show up for one another. If you nurture the bond it will last a lifetime.

143

....

When you're trying to make changes, you're going to hit
some resistance somewhere along the way. This is normal.
It doesn't mean you're failing; it means you're changing,
which is exactly what you want. So lean into it, breathe
deep, and continue taking action anyway. It will feel
hard, but remind yourself, "I'm changing and this is
what I want." It will get easier with time.

144

....

It doesn't make you a less amazing or caring individual
to choose not to support someone else in a way that will
drain you, whether that's emotionally, financially,
or in another way. You can send them love, wish them
the best, and be their cheerleader without giving up too
much of yourself or what's in your bank account.
Always listen to your gut and go with what feels right.
No one can argue with that.

145

....

If you want to make big changes in your life,
you have to change your mindset first. You literally
have to rewire your brain, and the only way to do
this is to choose, in each moment, to respond, act,
and think differently about what's happening.
Choose to respond positively. Choose to tell
yourself a new story. Choose to take a different action.
Every little choice you make adds up quickly.

146

....

Do you know what you need in your relationships?
Before someone can truly make you happy,
you have to understand what you desire and need,
and be able to give it to yourself first. A healthy
relationship with another person stems from having
a healthy relationship with yourself first. If you can't
make you happy, no one else will be able to.

147

. . . .

Your health and well-being should always be your number one priority, above everything and everyone else. Without your health, you're literally nothing. It can feel counter-productive to take a nap, go for a run, or do things that simply bring you joy when your to-do list is a mile long, but I promise you that taking this time will only help make things happen faster.

148

....

If you want to learn to get comfortable being
uncomfortable, then you have to get uncomfortable first.
When you're in that space, simply allow yourself to feel
all the feelings and physical sensations. The moment you
fight it, everything goes off-kilter. Breathe into those
feelings and sensations and continue taking action.
The feeling will pass in a matter of seconds if
you allow yourself to fully lean into and feel it.

149

. . . .

Sometimes you have to walk away from a stable relationship, the job that pays the bills, or another "secure" situation. When you live out of alignment with what you want and need, it will slowly eat at you, cause you stress, and depress you. You deserve amazing, joyful and passionate experiences. So check in with yourself and take the leap when it feels right.

150

....

Never apologize for any part of who you are. Apologize for hurting someone or doing something wrong, but you are who you are. For some people you may be alienating, abrasive, "too much," or hard to relate to. Do you really want those people in your circle? People that don't love you for who you are? No, probably not. So be who you are and allow the right people to come into your life after the wrong ones fall away.

151

Follow what feels right for you in the present. Maybe you think you should lift weights, but feel drawn to yoga. Maybe you think you should meditate, but feel drawn to paint. Your intuition is signaling what's right for you and what you need in this moment. Trust and follow it. Oftentimes, a random whim will lead you to something necessary and unexpected.

....

Sometimes people just know what they're talking about,
whether they have the credentials, education,
or experience you think it requires for them to know it.
This is wisdom and intuition at work. Listen with an
open mind, decide if it's relevant to you, keep what
works, and discard the rest. Don't write someone off
simply because of their age, education level, or any
other "qualification" they lack.

153

....

When you're feeling run down, don't push yourself to keep moving. Allow yourself the time and space to relax and recover. Reschedule commitments where you can, turn off your phone, and do something that rejuvenates your soul. Paint, take a walk, have lunch with a friend. It will make you happier and more productive in the long run to take this time for yourself and your spirit.

154

....

Stop making excuses. No matter what comes up, whether it's a real roadblock or perceived obstacle, there's always a way through or around. Brainstorm at least three alternates to your original plan and keep moving forward. Don't use these things as an excuse to throw in the towel and give up. Commit to finding another path!

155

....

Stop seeking love and joy from external sources like food, relationships, material goods, or titles. Ask yourself how you want to feel and how you can create that for yourself in this moment, with what you have, where you are, right now. You are 100% in control of your joy and happiness. Take ownership of that today.

156

....

Share your stories and your truth as much as possible
— the good, bad, embarrassing, and hilarious. We're
all so desperate for truth and connection in this world.
Don't try to be perfect or act like you're something you're
not. Just be you. Your truth and experiences will inspire
others, let them know they're not alone, and allow them
to connect with you on a much deeper level.

157

. . . .

Put time and energy into yourself as often as you can.
This may mean getting dressed up every day (just for
you), getting that massage, hiring a coach, buying a book
you want to read, taking a mental health day from work,
or learning something new. You're worth it. Every
penny and every minute. The more you do for you,
the more you can do for others.

158

....

Stop bending over backwards for people who have zero
respect for your time, talents, boundaries, expertise,
or kindness. Send them light and love, but stop catering
to their every whim. It doesn't make you less of a
generous, beautiful, and enlightened human being.
It means you place a higher value on yourself,
and that's the most important.

159

....

Take it one day, bill, phone call, and step at a time.
Whatever you're working towards, don't stress out about
the big picture and everything that needs to be done.
Take it one moment at a time. Are you okay in this
moment? The answer is likely yes, so feel your way into
that and continue to take one more step forward.

160

....

If you have an idea and it excites you to your core,
that's all that matters. It may take you time to find
others that get what you're so amped about, but that
doesn't mean there's not a place for it in this world.
This idea was entrusted to you because you're the person
capable and passionate enough to bring it to life.
Trust in that truth and move forward.

....

Just be honest about what you're feeling, even if you're not entirely sure what it means or why you feel the way you do. It's better to express yourself to the ones who love you than to try and act like nothing's wrong or stuff your feelings down. Allow yourself to feel what you feel, and don't let it become anything more than what it is.

. . . .

When you find yourself feeling impatient,
pause and come back to the present moment.
Appreciate where you are right now and focus on
how far you've come, not how far you have to go.
Give thanks and gratitude, love yourself as you are,
and celebrate the big and small milestones.

163

. . . .

When you find yourself drawn towards something you
want in the moment, but that will derail your goals or
make you feel crappy, remind yourself why you're doing
what you're doing. To be healthy? Keep up with your
kids? Live a long, impactful life? Remind yourself,
"I love myself more than I want this piece of chocolate."
Or, "I respect my dreams more than I want to
waste time on this activity."

164

....

Don't be one of those people who requires a
near-death experience or disease in order to awaken
to the reality that life is short and precious. Live with
a sense of urgency and allow that to guide you towards
doing what you love, connecting deeper, living with
purpose, and following your heart.

165

....

Wear what you want, dance how you dance, speak your truth, and just be yourself. If people don't like it, that's okay. Alienating others is a great sign that you're on the right path to living as your authentic self. It also means you're on the right path to finding your people and tribe, who will love you as you are and get you on every level.

....

If something's really important to you, then you'll make time for it, not excuses. Call the person you care about, create the time to get your workout in, or visit your family. Get really honest with yourself about where you're letting important people and things fall by the wayside in lieu of less important tasks on your to-do list.

167

....

If you want to experience more joy and positivity in
your life, you have to make it a practice. Every single day,
make the choice to respond positively to situations and
people. Speak positively, stay open minded, and expect
things to work out. Practice gratitude and appreciation
for what you have right now, and your level of
joy will increase instantly.

. . . .

Decide to stop being a victim. Instead, choose to be
the creator of your life. Rather than feeling like life is
happening to you, become a co-creator of your reality. If
something goes wrong or you're feeling down, choose to
look for solutions and creative ways to make the changes
you want in your life. You have everything you need to
create what you want; don't surrender to negativity.

169

....

Don't be afraid to do things by yourself.
Learn to love being in your own company and taking
yourself on dates. Go to the movies, have a meal, or do
something you really want, like attending a concert,
going to a play, or whatever else pulls at you.
If you want fulfilling relationships, you have to
learn to be content alone first. And besides, you're the
one person you have to spend your whole life with,
so you may as well make it a fulfilling relationship.

170

. . . .

It's never too late to go after your dream, no matter how big or unrealistic it may seem. Whether you're 20, 40, or 85, prioritize your dreams and living a life you love starting today. Just begin, and don't worry about what you think is the right age, income level, status, or anything else. Start to take little steps forward and you'll be on your way.

171

·················

When you're feeling stressed, pause and take a deep breath. Breathe slowly and deeply into your lungs and then exhale fully. Repeat, repeat, repeat. When we're stressed, we stop breathing or begin to take short breaths, which causes more tension. Deep breaths signal to our body that we're calm and everything's okay. Close your eyes and breathe. Everything will be just fine.

....

Break out of your current circle from time to time.
Sometimes the people we've known for long periods of
time begin to hold us back. They form an expectation
of who we're supposed to be based on who we were or
how our circle operates. If you want to live an amazing
life, you have to grow. Sometimes that means
you outgrow your circles, and that's okay.

173

....

Paint a picture of your perfect life and business, even
if you're unsure about every little detail, and especially
when you don't know how you'll make it happen.
Start with the vision so that you can be clear what
feelings, lifestyle, energy, and relationships you
want to have; then you can start making choices
and take action based on that vision.

174

....

Learn to listen to your body and what it's asking for.
Maybe you planned to work out like a crazy person this
week, but today you're feeling worn out, tired, and sore.
Take a break! As long as you're listening to your body and
not the resistance or excuses in your head, you're golden.
Your body will let you know when and what it needs.

175

....

Don't be afraid to reach out and connect with someone new. If you want to grow as a person, learn new things, have new experiences, and find your perfect tribe, you have to put yourself out there. You may be surprised to find that most people are open and inviting. People are starved for connection in this world, so take the time to say hello and make new friends.

176

. . . .

There's nothing wrong with you. Stop getting down on yourself and focusing on where you think you fall short. Instead, embrace where you are right now. Love yourself fully and expect no less from the people in your life. You are a beautiful and unique individual, and how you are right now in this moment is enough.

....

Every day, take one small step towards becoming the person you're meant to be. That might mean wearing lipstick, putting on an outfit you love, listening to certain music, or reading a book on a subject that fascinates you. It doesn't have to be big and outrageous. Slowly step into who you want to be and eventually, you'll step fully and completely into who you're meant to be.

178

....

Don't be afraid of alienating others or of rejection.
Work to see the positive side of the situation; by deterring
people and opportunities that don't belong in your life,
you're creating space for those that do. Celebrate each
time this happens and trust that something
(or someone) more fitting is on its way to you.

179

....

You don't need anything to give you courage, be
it alcohol or something else. Real courage means
being brave enough to put yourself out there, be
uncomfortable, and get vulnerable. It's the only way
to create real connection and to grow as a person.
How can you be more courageous today,
in your relationships or elsewhere?

....

It's okay to change your mind or change your plans,
as long as you communicate with the people involved.
Things come up and feelings change, and that's okay.
What's not okay is to just leave people hanging.
Speak your truth and apologize when necessary.
It's always better to be open and honest with others.

181

. . . .

Own your stories and the things that have
happened to you. They've made you the wonderful
person you are today. Don't be ashamed or embarrassed;
we all make mistakes. That's what makes us human,
and those truths are what help us connect on a
very deep level with others. Be real.

182

....

Walk your talk, always. If you're preaching
green living, clean eating, positivity, or any
other belief, be sure that you're taking your own
advice first. Lead by example, inspire others with
your life and work, and be a beacon of light in this world.
Don't just preach at or push others; show them the
benefits by being a poster child for your beliefs.

183

....

Introverts aren't weird and extroverts aren't annoying.
We're all just different, and that's perfectly okay.
Stop judging and labeling others just because they're not
like you. Take the time to learn something from them,
get to know who they are, and grow as an individual.
If you only know people like you, you'll never
expand as a person.

184

....

If you want to bring more joy into your life,
find the opportunities in every situation to make it
more fun and joyful. Turn the music on, choose
to smile, make a joke or laugh instead of yelling.
Joy and positivity are choices, ones that you have to
continue to make every single day. Ask yourself,
"How can I bring more joy into this moment?"

185

....

Stop caring so much what other people think; the only thing that matters is what you think. Is it right for you? Is it what you want? Do you like how that outfit looks on you? Awesome, roll with it. Trust yourself and your intuition, because you're the only person in this world who really knows what's right and best for you.

186

....

Your fears are not unique to you. Your experience of
them is, and your feelings surrounding them are valid,
but almost everyone in this world shares many of
the same fears. Breathe into them, and stay present
in your body and engaged in the physical sensations.
Get comfortable with the feelings it stirs up
and keep moving forward.

....

If you want to write, start writing. If you want to paint,
start painting. If you want to dance, start dancing.
Whatever you want to do, start doing it today!
Don't wait another day, week, month, or year to start
following your passions, learning what you want to learn,
or becoming who you want to be. What can you do
today to lean into your whims?

188

....

It's okay to not do the thing everyone else is doing,
especially when you really don't want to do it.
If you want to go home when everyone's going out,
awesome. If you want to go dancing when everyone
wants to go to bed early, go for it. Be yourself and
do what feels best for you in the moment.
You can't go wrong.

189

....

Don't contribute to gossip or stereotypes.
Find new ways to talk about people; use positivity,
truth, love, and compassion, or don't say anything at all.
It's not your business or place to discuss someone
else's life, relationships, habits, or choices.
Make it a rule not to say anything you wouldn't
say in front of the person in question.

190

....

Speak kindly to yourself, the same as you would with others. Don't assume a question you have is stupid, and don't get down on your younger self for the decisions you made. You're human, just like everyone else. How you speak about your actions and self has the same amount of, if not higher, impact on you as what others say to you.

191

....

If someone gets angry because you're doing what's
best for you, remember that it's their issue, not yours.
Maybe they feel jealous that you have the ability to act
on your own needs. Maybe they're resentful because they
never put themselves before others. Regardless of the
reason, keep doing what you're doing; they need
to sort it out themselves.

192

....

If you're not uncomfortable or experiencing some fear, you're probably not growing or making awesome changes in your life. Don't let fear stop you from moving forward; it will always be present, regardless of how far down the path of life you are or how successful you appear. Fear is normal. Feel it and keep moving.

193

....

Life isn't about sprinting to the finish line in record time, it's about the journey, and the journey requires you to learn some lessons and have some trying experiences on the way. Remember, there's always a bigger picture than what you're seeing in front of you. Stay positive, trust the process, and take good care of yourself.

194

....

All that matters is whether you feel in your bones that
something is right or wrong for your life. No one else's
experience, wisdom, or opinion is relevant. It's impossible
for anyone other than you to know what's best
for your life. You're living your life and you're
experiencing the world in your own unique way.
You get to decide for yourself.

. . . .

If you don't honor, enforce, and respect your own boundaries, no one else will. We teach others how to treat us by how we treat ourselves and how much we let them get away with. Stop allowing people into your life who are disrespectful, cruel, demanding, or anything along those lines. Take responsibility for your time and how you're treated.

196

....

Life is not black and white. It's full of shades of gray
and a wide range of beautiful colors. Don't limit yourself
by what others have deemed the rules of the game.
Just because something worked or didn't work for them,
doesn't mean it will or won't for you. Trust your intuition
and instincts and move forward accordingly.

....

Practicing an attitude of gratitude is about choosing to be grateful for the lessons, experiences, and gifts in every situation, and there's always a lesson! Even when we're in the midst of it, amazing things are happening to us and we're being pushed to grow, shift, and expand in new ways. Trust the process and stay positive.

198

. . . .

Ask for what you want as clearly as possible.
Other people can't give you what you want if they don't
know what it is. Stop expecting them to; nobody can read
your mind. Better yet, master the art of giving yourself
what you want so that others can easily follow suit. The
only person responsible for your happiness is you.

199

....

Setting boundaries means nothing unless you
actually honor them. You have to ask yourself,
"What's non-negotiable for me in this relationship
or situation?" Then you have to honor it.
We expect others to fall into line, but we're the
ones who have to set the boundary and walk
away from those that don't respect them.

200

. . . .

If you're feeling overwhelmed and stressed out, take a
moment to close your eyes, breathe deeply, and relax.
Take a time-out and just breathe. Focus on your breath,
be present in your body, and leave everything else
behind. Simple, quiet, and meditative moments like this
throughout your day will make a world of difference.

201

....

It's not your responsibility to change others or help them see the error of their ways. The only person you're responsible for is you. If you don't like someone's actions, eliminate them from your life or choose to lead by example. Focus on yourself and doing what you believe to be right; the rest will fall into place.

....

Be considerate of the animals and people that surround you. We're all in a shared space here. Yes, you have your own home, but the air, water, and natural resources belong to us all, animals included. You wouldn't walk into someone's house and trash their things, so why pollute their air or trash the environment? Work to be more aware of your impact and we'll all benefit.

. . . .

Resistance is normal as you work towards a goal,
especially when it's something you really need and want
to move to a new level. Do your best to push through the
resistance and move forward. All you have to do is take a
deep breath and take one small step forward. What can
you do to move through your resistance today?

204

It's easy to be the person passing judgment and giving advice on what someone should do in any situation. Take a moment to put yourself in their shoes. Is it really that easy? Is it really worth the energy and time? Is this really what you'd do yourself in that situation? Be supportive rather than judgmental.

205

. . . .

It's okay to say no. Sometimes you just don't want to do something or it's not for you. Maybe you have the time, but you'd rather spend it relaxing with your family or focusing on your self-care. There's nothing wrong or selfish about that. To be of better service to others and the world, we have to take care of ourselves first.

206

....

You're under no obligation to share what's happening for you or what's going on in your mind. Choose wisely whom you share with and protect what's most important to you. When change, big dreams, or deep desires are involved, others can muck things up with their opinions, expectations, or lack of understanding.

. . . .

Wherever you are right now, it's exactly where you need to be. Whatever you're experiencing right now, it's exactly what you need to be experiencing. You may not be able to see the lesson or the gift in it, but it's there, I promise you. You're learning, growing, shifting, changing, and becoming more of who you're truly meant to be.

208

....

You have to create an ecology that supports the life you want. Whether it's friendships, home environment, education, mentors, or experiences, if you don't have the right ecology in place, you won't be able to move forward. Start by truly loving and appreciating where you're at now, while also looking to see where you can begin shifting.

209

....

Stop expecting others to bring happiness into your life.
Feeling happy and fulfilled shouldn't be dependent on
anything or anyone outside yourself. Start with expressing
gratitude for what you have and taking a positive look at
everything in your life. It's not easy, but it's where
you have to begin if you want to feel joy.

210

. . . .

Immerse yourself in what you need to learn.
If you're working on your finances, health, or something
else, become a student of it. Read all the books and
articles you can find. Take notes. Watch documentaries
and movies. Go to free lectures or take online programs.
The only way to grow is to know, so get out
there and start learning.

211

....

Take time to celebrate your accomplishments
and how far you've come. Stop thinking only about
what's left to do or where you're not. What have you
done in the last six months? Where were you a year ago,
and how have you changed in positive ways?
What do you have to be grateful for? If you want to
thrive, compare yourself to yourself and no one else.

212

....

Just because a lot of people are a certain way
doesn't mean you have to be that way. It's okay to
be the quiet one, to dress differently, or to have totally
different interests. It's also okay to be loud, or dress in
the latest trends, so long as you're doing it for you and
what you want, not for others. You're perfect as is,
so own it and stay true to you.

213

....

Instead of wondering what you can get out of every
experience, relationship, encounter, or opportunity, ask
what you can give. How can you be of service to others?
How can you support, love, or uplift someone else?
How can you create a better conversation or community?
Being of service serves everyone involved, especially you.

214

. . . .

Sometimes we just need a time-out. It doesn't mean that
we need to make drastic changes or that we don't love the
people around us; it simply means that we need a break.
Time to step back and reflect, to go inward and listen
to what we really need and desire, to recover from
the stress and demands of our daily lives.

. . . .

Don't let a mistake, error of judgment,
or poor choice haunt you all your life. We're all human
here, and that means we make mistakes. When those
negative feelings come up, tell yourself you forgive
yourself and you love yourself, and release the energy
attached. Breathe in deeply, exhale fully, and say,
"I love you, I forgive you, I release you."
Then move forward. Repeat as often as you need.

216

. . . .

While it's awesome to have people you can talk through things with, you also need to take the space to really hear your intuition. When we ask for advice from multiple people, it's usually due to a lack of trust and faith in ourselves, our intuition, and the Universe. Take a moment and check in. What feels right to you?

217

Everything in life is a journey and a process.
You have to start somewhere! You have to make a
choice to change before anything else, and then?
You have to take baby steps and continue to choose
this new direction every single day, over and over again.
What one thing can you do now to start the process?

218

....

Sometimes you have to repeat your boundaries
to people time and time again. Don't let anyone make
you feel bad for standing firm in what works for you.
If they don't know how to honor themselves and
their own boundaries, they'll expect you to break
down on yours. If it's what you need, honor it
regardless of what they say or do.

219

....

If something's not working, it's neither good nor bad;
it's just not working. If you've given it adequate
time to kick in or to see results and nothing's happening,
then stop trying to force it. Get creative, read a new
book, or try someone else's recommendation.
Take a look at the options and trust your intuitive
response. You'll know what to try next.

220

....

It can be hard to try and find your path when people in your life have become accustomed to having a say in it, such as your parents, family, friends, maybe even peers, a coach, or a mentor. At some point, we have to break away and create space to try and experiment. To do what we feel called to do. Make that space when you need it.

221

. . . .

Don't give up on yourself. Whatever your goal or dream, just focus on the next step. Even if you mess up, simply recommit and refocus. What can you do right now to move even the slightest bit closer to what you want? What can you learn today in order to be more prepared and equipped? Baby steps. Daily choices. You've got this.

222

....

Life is full of ebbs and flows. Trust that when things are slow or not going the way you'd like, there's something positive coming your way. Things are in the works, the Universe is shifting, and all the seeds you plant will come to bloom in their right time. Take care of yourself, trust in the process, and stop trying to force things.

223

. . . .

Be kind and compassionate to everyone you come across.
People who are angry, hostile, and demanding often need
the most love and compassion. You don't know their
story, and while it doesn't excuse poor treatment
or behavior, it explains why they act the way they do.
Don't keep them in your life, but send them
healing light and love.

224

....

Experiment with life! Try something you've never tried
before, such as a class, a restaurant, or a route home
from work. When we experiment, we allow ourselves to
explore what we love, who we are, and what we really
want. Don't allow yourself to get stuck in a rut.
Pick something random and see how it goes.

225

. . . .

Learn to live with less and simplify your life and belongings where you can. This creates the space for new people, things, and experiences to come in, but also to create the stillness, mental focus, and quiet to better hear and heed your intuition. If something is unnecessary, doesn't bring you joy, or bogs you down, eliminate it.

226

....

Make it a point to honor your commitments to yourself as much as you would to someone else. If you block off time for your morning routine, creative practice, money management, workouts, or anything else, honor it! Your life, happiness, health, and well-being depend on it. Show yourself some respect by showing up for your own commitments.

227

....

Always remember that you're human, no matter how
successful you get. You're going to make mistakes,
change your mind, and find yourself on a new
journey of self-discovery for as long as you live.
It's okay to be human; in fact, people love people
that are human. So show up. Speak your truth and
share your journey. It's needed.

228

. . . .

No matter how small your progress is, you have to
acknowledge all of it. Celebrating the little wins,
accomplishments, shifts, and gains is so important
to building a life you love. If you don't take the time
to express gratitude and appreciation for what
you've done in your life, you'll never be satisfied
and will continue to stay stuck.

229

....

You're capable of providing yourself with all the love, happiness, attention, and connection you desire. All you have to do is ask yourself what you want to experience and how you can create it in your life. You don't need someone or something else. Get creative and be your own number one supporter for all your needs and desires.

....

If you want to supercharge your life, relationships,
and work, allow yourself to experience more fear.
Most people work to avoid fearful situations at all costs,
but avoidance leads to a life that lacks purpose, passion,
and fulfillment. Experiencing fear is a prerequisite to
any type of positive change in your life!

231

....

It's normal for things to change over the years, whether it's your preferences, opinions, beliefs, or taste buds. Don't be afraid to like something you've claimed to hate for years. You're not required to stay the same! More importantly, you don't want to box yourself in. Allow yourself the freedom to change as it suits you.

232

....

Never take advice from someone who doesn't have what you desire. It doesn't matter if they're your best friend, trusted family member, or a mentor; if they haven't successfully achieved what you want for yourself, they're in no position to give advice to you on how to achieve it for yourself. Be cautious and selective about whom you allow to guide you on your journey.

233

. . . .

This moment is the only moment that you have and this is who you are right now. Rather than trying to live in a past or future version of yourself, be here now. See who you really are in a loving and compassionate light. You don't have to like it, but you have to love and care for yourself as you are right now.

234

....

Believe in the possibilities for yourself. The only thing
between where you are now and having, creating,
finishing, and completing those seemingly impossible
dreams is your belief that they're not impossible.
If someone out there is doing or has done it,
you can do it too. If no one out there is doing
or has done it, you can still do it.

235

....

Redefining how you see a situation or experience is the key to experiencing miracles in your life. Ask how you can see things differently or how you can experience them in a more positive light. Gratitude transforms even the harshest of situations. The more dedicated you are to redefining your experience, the happier you'll be.

236

....

Don't be afraid to speak your truth. People may not want to hear it or may not agree with you, but it's yours to speak. Holding back is unhealthy and leads to lack of fulfillment, joy, connection, and passion. Speak up! Whether it's that you have a differing opinion, want someone to know how you feel, or think something wrong is happening, be brave with your voice. You owe it to yourself and others.

. . . .

Rest when you need to rest. While society may push that busy is better, it's not. Take the time and make the space to be still, take naps, walk aimlessly in nature, read, think, explore. Choose things that refill your well and make you feel fulfilled and happy. Rest is as important as action in any situation. Prioritize it every single day.

238

....

Sometimes as we work towards a goal we realize it's not for us, and that's okay! If you take a hard look at what you wanted to create and it hasn't manifested yet, you might find that you really don't want it that badly, or maybe it's not a priority. Free yourself from the obligation to work towards something you no longer desire.

239

....

Give yourself permission to be more adventurous in
life! This could be anything from ordering something
different at a restaurant to traveling alone to a new place.
Adventure challenges us to get uncomfortable;
it broadens our experiences, teaches us new things
(about ourselves and the world), refills our spiritual
well, and peaks our creativity.

240

....

Always give people the benefit of the doubt, but if
something feels off, trust your intuition. Everything and
everyone is made from energy, so if you get a weird vibe
or a sense that something isn't working or won't work,
trust yourself. Learning to trust your intuition is essential
to building a business, career, relationship,
or life that you truly love.

241

. . . .

When you're feeling overwhelmed by life, it's important
to focus on and create wins. Celebrate the things you
accomplished last week, even if it's just getting the
laundry done. Choose something you want to do and
commit to taking action on it every day for the next
week. Even if it's small steps forward, celebrate
that you're making progress, because you are!

242

....

Sometimes things don't go the way we expect them to. Instead of seeing it as a failure, see it as an opportunity to re-evaluate your goals, what's working and what's not, and what your next steps should be. Working towards any big goal requires openness, resilience, and an ability to shift as the path changes in front of you.

243

....

If someone wants to be around you even though they're in a bad mood, it doesn't mean you have to spend time with them. You're responsible for protecting your own energy and doing what's necessary for your happiness. That might mean creating space when someone else's energy starts to bring yours down.

244

. . . .

Go ahead and make the change you want to make
in your life. Try out the new wardrobe, rock the new
hairstyle, read something different, or start painting and
playing guitar. You don't need any other reason than "this
is what feels good to me right now." Trust your urges;
they'll never lead you astray. We all shape-shift over
the years. Be open and embrace it fully.

245

....

You're the only one who knows your truth. A coach, friend, mentor, guide, or teacher can help you to see things you may not, but if someone tells you something about yourself, your actions, or your life and it doesn't resonate, discard it immediately. Only keep the thoughts and advice that resonate for you. If their words don't spark an aha moment, don't think twice about it.

246

....

Regardless of what's going on in your life or if someone is bringing you down, you're still responsible for the energy you bring into every situation. These are only explanations, not excuses, to treat others poorly. Do what you need to do to create shifts and show up positively, even if that's a simple shift in your perspective on the situation or experience.

247

. . . .

Love the people in your life as deeply and
compassionately as you're able. See them for who they
are, accept their flaws and shortcomings, and allow them
the space to be who they want to be. This includes how
you treat yourself! You deserve the best love in
the world, and it should start with you.

248

. . . .

Adopt the mantra, "It's not up to me; it's up to my intuition." Rely on this divine source of wisdom, knowing, and guidance over the rationalizations of the mind. Your intuition knows, while your mind and ego fear and complicate. Trust that intuitive hit or gut feeling always and you won't be lead astray.

. . . .

There's wisdom in the concept of looking back at your youth and seeing what you were passionate about, what tugged at your heart and soul, and whom you were inspired by. We're drawn to certain things and people for a reason, either because we want to do what they're doing or something similar, or because there's something in us that we see in them. What were you drawn to?

250

....

Do something pointless today. Go for a walk to nowhere, have a TV marathon in your pajamas, doodle a cartoon of your dog, or just drive around aimlessly. Do something that doesn't have any other intention than relaxing, getting out of your head, and rejuvenating your spirit. Pointless has a point, which is to make you feel awesome.

....

Don't shift your natural energy levels depending on whom you're around; stay true to what works for you. If you're high energy, be high energy. If you're low energy, be low energy. Trying to be something you're not will drain you, cause stress, and make you feel out of alignment with your truth. Just be you. You're perfect.

252

....

If you want to create a habit, you have to take it one day at a time. Every morning, recommit yourself to what you intend to do. No excuses. Looking at it one day at a time takes away the feeling that it's a long and painful process, or that you're trying to overhaul an area of your life. Every day, commit. Take the action you need to take without thoughts attached to it, and you'll get there before you know it!

. . . .

Actions speak louder than words, so what are
your actions telling the people you love? You may say
I love you, but do you show it? You may say it's
important, but are you actually making it a priority?
You may say you're trying, but are you actually taking
the steps involved? Strive to let your actions do
all the talking, clearly and honestly.

254

....

Don't engage in negativity. Sometimes people will
try to push your buttons, be passive aggressive,
and attempt to bring you down to their level.
Send them light and love, don't take it personally,
and don't engage. Excuse yourself from the
conversation, remove them from your life,
or create distance where you can.

255

. . . .

While it's nice to be supported and have people agree with what you're doing, if you're really looking to live an amazing, fulfilling, and authentic life, you'll eventually find yourself in a situation where no one's on your side. So long as this choice resonates for you on a gut level, that's all you need to move forward. Trust yourself.

256

. . . .

Life isn't about perfection; it's about love, passion, fulfillment, creativity, connection, and experience. Stop fretting over things that don't truly matter. You're perfect and beautiful and amazing as you are right now. Nothing external needs to change for you to be happy and start living a life you love. Shift your energy to a place of gratitude for this moment.

257

....

Do something every single day that scares and challenges
you or pushes you into the realm of being uncomfortable.
If we're not uncomfortable or experiencing a healthy
dose of fear, we're not growing. When you stop growing,
you become stagnant. Make it a point to do something
daily that pushes you to grow.

258

. . . .

When life gets busy, focus on the present moment.
Just do the task at hand. Just be with the person
in front of you. Drive the drive. Walk the walk.
Take the next step, and stay focused on that alone.
The easiest way to work through busyness is to stay
present. You'll be more efficient and productive,
but also far less stressed in the process.

259

....

Wear what you like, not what's trendy.
Do what you want, not what everyone else is doing.
Speak your mind; don't just join in with the crowd.
Find yourself and honor that person fully. Be unique,
different, and weird. Don't follow along with anything
unless it really, truly speaks to you.

260

....

Work to reach a deeper level of vulnerability with the people you love. Speak your truth, share what you feel, and be open about your dreams. Sit with the uncomfortable feeling of being exposed and keep your heart open. Even if you're not well received, stay open. The more open you stay, the easier it becomes to create deep, loving connections.

261

....

Let people help you. Sure, you could probably do it all yourself, but you don't have to. Ask for help. Reach out to family and friends. Hire a coach or mentor. Join a class or program. Read a book or attend a lecture. Learn from people who've already done it. Accept a helping hand from people who offer it. You deserve to be supported.

262

....

If you want to experience change, you have to
start by being honest with yourself about where
you're at now, and why that's not working for you
and the life you want to live. It's only when we're present
and honest with ourselves that we can start to lovingly
shift the situation. Change doesn't come in the
future; it comes from this moment.

263

....

It's never okay to be abusive with another person,
even if they're acting abusive towards you. Choose to be
and see the light in the situation. Take a deep breath,
create space when needed, stay positive, and don't sink to
their level. It's not your job to make them see the light;
it's your job to be the light in your own life.

....

When things get stressful or you're feeling overwhelmed, just take a deep breath and breathe into the areas of your body that feel stressed. Imagine that you're breathing light and love into that space, and clearing out the negative energy on the exhale. Breathe, love, and release. Repeat as often as needed.

265

....

Just because you got hurt by someone once
(or many times) doesn't mean you should close your
heart off to love and connection. As painful as these
experiences are, they're part of life and part of growing
as a person. Look for the lessons, get clearer on what
you want and don't want, and let it crack you open
to more love rather than closing you off.

266

....

Listen to your body. If it needs more rest, create the space to rest. If it needs more energy, adjust your diet to create it. If it craves movement, find a way to move it that feels best for you. Your body contains all the wisdom you need to care for it properly; you just have to take the time to listen. More importantly, act on what you need.

267

....

Sometimes you have to venture into the unknown
to build the life you deeply desire. It can be scary,
sometimes hard, and oh so uncomfortable, but it's worth
it. Every tear, fear-filled step, hard lesson, unexpected
turn, and everything in between — it's all worth it.
Breathe deep, be kind to yourself, trust the
process, and keep moving.

268

....

You never overcome fear; you simply learn to get
cozy with it. Fear will always be present in your life,
so long as you continue to push yourself towards a goal
or constant personal growth. The more you push yourself,
the more comfortable you get being uncomfortable,
and the easier it will be to cozy up to fear and
use it as fuel for the journey.

269

. . . .

If something doesn't feel right to you (or for you),
regardless of how big of an expert the person saying it is,
discard it. Listen when you feel compelled to and it feels
right for you and your life. You're the only expert
on anything related to you, so trust in your expertise.
Listen to your intuition above all else, always.

270

....

It's important to take space from things in our life.
Relationships, businesses and careers, obligations,
routines, homes, etc. When you take space from
something and tune out all the noise that goes along
with it, you gain a fresh perspective. You really see what's
working and what isn't, tune into your intuition,
and start making real changes.

271

....

Try not to worry so much about the big picture, full plan, how to get it done, or all the details in between. Just start. If you feel a pull towards something or have a passion, just lean into it. Take a little step forward, try something, experiment, play around. By taking action, you'll naturally find yourself on the path to building a life around what you love.

272

. . . .

What makes you different is what makes you special.
The very reason you feel you don't fit into the world
is your greatest gift. Embrace what's different, weird,
special, and unique about you! The sooner you do,
the sooner others will follow suit. Show up fully
and don't filter who you are. You're amazing
and you deserve to be seen.

273

....

Change doesn't have to be big, overwhelming, chaotic,
or jarring. It can just be. When you stay fully present
and focused on the moment you're in, life becomes less
bumpy. Massive changes feel seamless, stress reduces,
and you're able to flow forward with ease and grace.
Try just being in the moment you're in, nowhere else.

274

. . . .

What can you do to be of service right now?
Who can you reach out to with love and light?
Where can you offer support to someone in need?
How can you bring joy into the life of someone who
needs it? Get in the practice of giving with only the
intention to give, support, and be of service.
It's the fastest way to joy and fulfillment.

275

....

Some days are necessary mental health days and involve staying in bed until noon, wearing yoga pants all day, and eating chocolate tarts before 10 am. As long as you're listening to your body and desires, rather than avoiding or stuffing a feeling of emptiness, you're all good. It's more than okay to slow down, treat yourself, and do what feels best.

. . . .

No matter what's happening in your life, you can always choose to be happy. You choose happiness by accepting what is, as it is. You choose happiness by responding positively. You choose happiness by being grateful for the good in every situation. What will you choose right now?

277

....

If you're lucky enough to have someone in your
life that loves and supports you deeply, make sure
you take the time to nurture that relationship.
Do what you need to do to show them they're loved
and appreciated. Don't take for granted that you have
this person in your life, regardless of how deep the
love or how long the relationship.

278

....

Be enthusiastic about everything, because life itself is truly a miracle. When you look at even the most mundane task with enthusiasm, you'll increase your joy, get through it with ease, and have more energy for everything else. Joy, happiness, and enthusiasm are choices. Would you rather be miserable, or would you prefer to have an awesome life?

279

....

Closing out a chapter of your life, a relationship that's no longer serving you, or anything that needs to be laid to rest can open up so much space for amazing things to manifest. Take the time to do the necessary work. Clean, declutter, forgive, release, reorganize, shift, say goodbye, close it out, change it up. It's so worth the effort!

280

....

Fall in love with your life and everything in it.
When you're truly grateful for what you have,
you generate a deep level of love, respect, appreciation,
and adoration for the blessings that you have.
It's easier to focus on the bad, less than, or what's
missing, but falling in love with what you have
brings you far more joy and fulfillment.

281

．．．．．．．．．．．．．．．

Never forget that life is short and precious.
Always say how you feel, make time for the people
and things that matter, and take good care of yourself.
Don't save it for later or expect there will be more time;
assume this is your only chance. Let a sense of urgency
guide you to creating a more fulfilling life.

. . . .

Work on loving yourself as you are right now.
That might mean sending love to your thighs, being
compassionate about your lack of progress in a certain
area, or reminding yourself that you're an awesome
human being. Whatever it is, sit with yourself and express
love as you would towards someone you really care about.
Work to become your own best friend.

283

. . . .

There's always a deeper layer to your desires.
When you think about the thing, job, person,
or experience you want, why do you want it?
What do you really want to feel from gaining it?
How will your life improve? Where will you be
more joyful? Let these questions guide you deeper
into why you really desire what you desire.

284

. . . .

Take responsibility for your health by connecting with your body. Start by tuning in and asking what it craves, desires, or needs in this moment. Rest? Hydration? A big salad? Some sunshine and fresh air? As you begin to listen to your body, you'll start to make healthier choices, both in and out of the kitchen.

285

. . . .

Take responsibility for the things you do. If you hurt someone's feelings, apologize. If you made a mistake, own up to it and make it right. If you damaged someone else's property, leave a note. If you can't make it to a commitment, call and let them know. Be considerate of those that your actions have affected or will affect, always.

286

....

The risks of keeping things to yourself can be far greater than putting yourself out there. You may never get the chance to tell someone you love them. You may never mend relationships with family, set boundaries at work, or get exactly what you want. Don't set yourself up to always wonder what could have been! Speak your truth and see what happens.

287

....

Be respectful of other people's opinions.
We're all different, with varying values, beliefs,
backgrounds, and lives. That means that whatever the
issue at hand, no one's actually right. How can anyone
be right when we're all so different? When our beliefs
vary so greatly? Be true to what you believe,
but be respectful of those who may disagree.

288

....

Try not to let proving something to someone else be your motivation to make changes in life. More often than not, that's a false sense of motivation that will die out over time because it's not connected to a true why — as in why, on the deepest level, do you desire this change? Why does it matter to you?

289

....

Always be honest with the people in your life.
Not wanting to hurt someone's feelings is no reason
to tell a lie, no matter how little you think it may be.
It's far better to build relationships that are based on
truth, trust, and honest connections. If you don't want
to get into it, find something truthful to say,
but don't lie because it's easier.

290

....

It's okay to say no, be unavailable, or bow out of events
that are important to others. If you really want to show
up and be there for them, take care of yourself first.
Do what you need to do to be happy and healthy.
People who truly love and support you will understand.
Just be sure to extend them the same understanding.

. . . .

Don't define yourself by the things you own
or the titles you hold. Don't define yourself by the
relationships you have and the role you play within them.
Don't define yourself by your successes or your failures.
Strive to be open to growth and change, to be kind,
joyful, and compassionate, to trust the Universe,
and to show up fully.

292

. . . .

If something happened to you that affects your ability to show up in this world as a whole, happy, and healthy person, it needs to be dealt with. Whether that's cutting the energetic cord, releasing material possessions, talking to a therapist, or journaling for hours, deal with it. It's not worth living life less than 100% engaged.

293

....

Take the time to appreciate and honor the people in your
life that matter. Send a card, call them on the phone,
or make extra effort to let them know that they're loved
and appreciated. Say thank you, let them know you
notice what they do, and always give praise, credit,
or acknowledgement where it's due. This is how
you keep them happy and in your life.

294

....

The world and everyone in it is simply reflecting your beliefs back to you. If you believe life is a struggle, the Universe will present you with experiences that reinforce that belief. If you believe you're always being supported, you will be presented with the same experiences, but you will see them in a more positive light. What's being reflected back to you right now?

295

. . . .

No one's as impressive as they seem. We're all just doing
the best we can, making mistakes, learning, growing, and
seeking out love, connection, fulfillment, and peace.
Just because someone's more successful or famous
than you are doesn't mean they're not human.
We're all the same — never forget that.

296

....

Faith is about trusting that you're being given exactly what you truly need, regardless of whether or not you understand how it's serving you in that moment. Sometimes there's a lesson to be learned before you get what you desire or there's something so much better in store for you, if you can just keep on moving forward.

. . . .

Create more space in your calendar for yourself.
You don't have to fill every moment with interaction
or things to do. Work on just being alone and being
with yourself. Many people constantly fill their time
because they're afraid of being alone with their own
thoughts. Get comfortable with yourself and
learn to be your own best friend.

298

. . . .

Be conscious of the fact that this world is a shared space.
Your energy and actions have an effect on everyone and
everything around you. Remember that we share the
earth, water, air, and energy of this Universe with
each other and every other living thing. How
are you showing up in this shared space?
What shared outcome are you contributing to?

299

. . . .

Be kind to yourself in this moment, no matter what's happening. No matter if you're not where you think you should be in your life, body, relationships, or career. How can you expect to get anywhere when you have someone constantly cutting you down? Become your own cheerleader and best friend. You could use it.

300

....

Change your routine and try something different with a focus on self-care. Read fiction instead of self-help. Take a bubble bath instead of a shower. Take a walk in nature instead of hitting the gym. Bring more beauty, relaxation, love, and comfort into your routine where you can. It makes a world of difference.

301

. . . .

When things start going really well, it's common to
self-sabotage. We get used to a certain level of finances,
love, success, and connection. When we push past that,
it's not uncommon to do something that brings us back
to what's comfortable. When things start going well,
simply breathe into and accept the discomfort.
It will become comfortable soon enough.

302

....

Become a self-care maven. Start by determining what that means for you. What does daily decadence look like in your life? What would it look like to treat yourself like the finest person you've ever dated? To woo yourself? Care for yourself? Nourish yourself? Make a list of ideas and start implementing at least one thing right now!

....

Sometimes people hurt us, mistreat us, or make us feel bad. While it's crappy, it's also no excuse to do the same to them in return. Yes, relationships are a two-way street, but are you keeping your side clean and well maintained? Are you showing up fully, or letting things slack because of what they are or aren't doing? Be honest.

304

. . . .

Listen to your body. We may believe that being stressed out and exhausted and having an upset stomach is the norm of a busy life, but that doesn't mean it's actually normal. It's not normal to be tired and feel crappy all day, every day. It's not normal to need stimulants for energy. Your body is trying to tell you it needs something; make the space to listen and find out what.

305

....

Life's too short to worry about things that don't really matter. What's actually important to you? Making a difference? Depth and connection? Spirituality? Service? Get clear on who and what really matters to you and stop wasting time and energy on the things and people that don't.

306

....

Detach yourself from outcomes that are super specific.
Instead, focus on what you desire to feel from the thing
you want specifically. Use the mantra, "Let it be easy, let
it be right, let it be soon, thank you." Allow the Universe
the opportunity to bring you exactly what you desire,
in exactly the right way, at exactly the right time.

307

....

Life's too short to spend in a relationship of any kind
that doesn't deeply fulfill and satisfy you. Whether it's
romantic, a friendship, or a family relationship, if it's not
feeling good, it's not worth the time and energy.
Create the space from those relationships, or do
the work necessary to make them work. You deserve
connection and fulfillment, always.

308

....

When you truly learn to live in the moment, it may seem like your emotions are broken. Life simply starts moving forward with ease and grace. It's seamless, you're more even keeled, and you don't get fazed or stressed out as easily. Any time you catch yourself elsewhere, gently bring yourself back to the present.

....

Love and respect the ones you're with. Give them your full attention, love them as best you can, express what needs to be expressed, and prioritize their needs. Don't take them for granted. Life is short and relationships require ongoing nurturing. It can be easy to let love fade, but it's worth the effort to keep it strong.

310

. . . .

The best way to build a life you love is to start by
appreciating and fully participating in the life you have
now. Show up fully, engage with whom you have in front
of you, do the best work you can, appreciate the job,
and thank the Universe for the gifts in your life.
Like attracts like, so like where you're at.

311

....

Always look for the good in each person, situation, and experience. Even if you can't find it, remind yourself that everything is happening for a reason, you're being supported, and things always work out in the end. You don't have to see how it's going to turn out to know that; you just have to have faith and trust, and learn to surrender.

312

....

Just because everyone else is having a good time
or wants to do something doesn't mean you have to.
It's okay to want time and space to be alone, or to prefer
to spend time one-on-one rather than in groups.
Honor what's true for you and what would make
you happiest. You don't have to be like everyone
else, so honor your needs.

313

. . . .

Find the routines, processes, systems, and tools that work for you and stick with them. It doesn't matter what changes in technology, what becomes trendy in the moment, or what anyone else does; it only matters what works best for you. It's okay to do things differently, so long as you're happy with the outcome and results.

314

....

It's important to do pointless activities — the ones that seem unproductive, random, and sometimes selfish, like drawing, watching documentaries in your PJs, and taking walks to nowhere. These pointless and unproductive activities are vital to our health, happiness, and creativity because they refill the well and refuel our souls.

315

....

Meet new people as often as you can.
Say hi to someone in an elevator, volunteer at a
retirement home, be friendly and open. Everyone has an
interesting story to share, and you never know whom
you'll meet: an important connection on a plane, a new
friend waiting in line at the coffee shop, or maybe the
love of your life at the Laundromat. Be open, kind,
and a lover of all people. It's worth the energy.

316

....

At any moment, you can fully embody the
person that you want to become. You can be sexy, joyful,
passionate, playful, successful, abundant, and expressive.
You just have to make the choice. Any time you say,
"I wish I was…" just make the choice to become it.
Right now. You have that power, always.

317

....

It's okay to say no. To your boss, significant other,
mother-in-law, or anyone else asking something of you
that's out of alignment with who you are, what you want
to create, or what you believe to be best. You owe nothing
more than "it doesn't feel right." There are consequences
to our actions, but staying in alignment with your truth
is one of the most important things you can do.

318

....

If you let other's actions or words affect your happiness,
then you've given away your power. Yes, words can sting,
but you have a choice in whether you let them affect how
you feel about yourself or your life. Hurtful words
are a reflection of the person's own issues and troubles,
not a truth about you or a reflection of your worth.

. . . .

We lose our fire, glow, and magnetism when we lose our playfulness. Life is supposed to be fun, joyful, and filled with love and connection. When you close off and get too serious, you miss out on the beauty of this life and world. Where are you closing off or taking things too seriously? How can you create more playfulness instead?

320

. . . .

Speak up when you need something that you're
not receiving in any relationship, be it at work, in
friendships, with family, or with your significant other.
If you feel lonely, disconnected, ignored, unappreciated,
or anything else, speak your truth. Your feelings are valid,
and when shared with kindness and truth,
they're more likely to be understood.

321

....

If you want to take control of your life and move it in a more positive direction, you have to get honest about what's not working. Where are you wasting time on things that don't matter? Who is in your life that shouldn't be? Where aren't you as responsible as you should be? Getting honest leads to making positive changes, so begin right now.

322

....

Always take the high road. Be professional and remain respectful in your words and actions, even when someone is out of line or treating you poorly. Be a person of integrity and class, and don't ever sink to their level. Reacting to someone at the same level is easy, but it won't get you anywhere. Stay calm, and stay on the high road.

323

....

Being of service is one of the most fulfilling things you
can do, whether that's tithing to charities each year,
fundraising, volunteering, giving back, or simply helping
someone who needs support. If we all choose to live a life
of service, to the degree that suits us, this world will
be a much more loving, beautiful place.

324

. . . .

Instead of getting angry with someone who wrongs you, take a moment to see them for who they really are: a person who's probably having a rough time right now. Even if they just seem like a mean individual, there are things at play you can't see. Always give people more kindness than they may seem to deserve in the moment.

325

....

Whether you believe life is a struggle, all guys are jerks,
and things never go your way, or you believe that
you're always being guided and supported,
people are generally good and kind, and life is filled
with possibility, the Universe will continually present
you with experiences that prove you right.
What will you choose to see in your life?

326

. . . .

Any strong spiritual practice begins with a strong
connection to your intuition. If you're unable to
feel your way through any opportunity, decision,
or choice, then you're not connecting with this incredible
part of yourself. Your intuition is in your body,
not your mind. Take a moment to breathe into your
body and see what comes up for you.

327

....

The more faith you have in the Universe, the more frequently it will deliver. When you trust that something that went wrong was meant to happen, your faith will be rewarded with a positive outcome that truly serves you. Maybe not in the moment, but sooner than expected, and in amazing ways you can't even imagine right now.

328

....

Venting is a transfer of negative energy onto another person. If you need to talk it out, talk it out, but how can you diffuse the negative energy first? A good workout? Screaming into a pillow? Writing it out in your journal? Take responsibility for the energy you bring into a conversation and do what you need to do first.

329

....

Make a practice of living in this moment, the one right
in front of you. Fully engage in what's happening,
whom you're with, and where you're at. When you master
the art of living in the moment, life is easy, graceful,
and seamless. There are no jarring transitions,
life is less stressful, and it's easy to navigate the
sometimes rough waters of this world.

330

....

Be the kind of person that shows up, delivers,
and follows through on their word, regardless of whether
it matters, there is a firm deadline, or anyone will know.
Do it for yourself, and if you're not perfect at it right
now, strive to do better, one promise, commitment,
obligation, and deadline at a time.

331

. . . .

As you go about your day, check in with your body. What does it desire and crave? While you might think that it's chocolate and wine, maybe what it really needs is a bubble bath, some cool green juice, and a good night's rest. Don't let your brain mask your body's true desires with what it thinks you want; really tune in and listen.

332

. . . .

Take the time to deal with those tasks, issues,
or obstacles that are falling by the wayside and causing
added stress in your life. Look at your finances,
call the person you need to call, sit down and pay the
bills, or send out the packages. Once you do, you'll feel
lighter and more focused, even if the thing you
need to do isn't fun or enjoyable.

333

....

Nothing feels as amazing as being seen, loved, and adored for exactly who you are, but you can never experience this within a relationship if you're unable to show up fully, vulnerably, and authentically. It's scary, and it's absolutely possible you might get hurt along the way, but there's no other way to create those deep connections.

334

. . . .

Take a look at your life right now and ask yourself,
"Where am I feeling drained, dissatisfied, and unhappy?"
Then ask yourself how you can bring more pleasure and
joy into those moments so that you can experience more
joy and fulfillment, without having to make massive
shifts in your life. Pleasure and joy are prerequisites for
a life you love, not the other way around.

335

. . . .

Change doesn't have to be hard or scary.
It can be fun and exciting, even if it seems like you're
taking a step back. Embrace newness with open arms,
curiosity, and enthusiasm. What's there to be learned?
What are the positive feelings that come with the new?
Where can you go from here? Change is a part
of life; work to embrace it.

336

....

It may seem like you don't have time for self-care,
but it's worth every extra moment you can give it.
Take a bath, read that book, go for a walk,
cuddle with someone you love. You'll feel replenished,
energized, joyful, and relaxed. This leads to more
productivity and less stress. Self-care is the fuel
for your tank; don't neglect it.

. . . .

When things go wrong, take a step back and ask yourself,
"How big a deal is this, really?" When the Internet goes
down, your car needs repairs, or something simply falls
through, is it really, truly worth stressing over?
Allow things to just be what they are, and allow
yourself to just feel what you feel, so that you can
move on to greater things more quickly.

338

....

Be kind and compassionate to everyone, including that one person that constantly triggers you, rubs you the wrong way, or tries to egg you on. People that act this way typically do so out of a deep need for love and acceptance, because of old wounds, or because they're insecure. It doesn't mean you put up with it, but you can at least send some love and compassion their way.

339

. . . .

Never let someone tell you that you can't do something you really desire. Never, ever. If your heart longs for it, your soul clings to it, and your intuition screams for it, then it will happen. But you have to trust first and continue to take action, regardless of the naysayers. You were given this dream or goal; it's your responsibility to honor that.

340

. . . .

Let go of your age. Whether you're in your 20s, 30s, 40s, 50s, 60s, or beyond, stop defining yourself by the number of years your body has existed on this planet. Just release the number and allow yourself to be who you are, where you are, and with whatever life experience you have, rather than limiting yourself.

341

....

Relationships should add to your life, not complete it.
If you find yourself feeling lost, incomplete, or empty
because you're not in a relationship, you need to focus
on the relationship you have with yourself. It can hurt
to lose another, but it shouldn't leave you feeling
empty or incomplete. Learn to fill yourself,
love yourself, and be whole yourself.

342

. . . .

Everything doesn't have to go perfectly; it's still going
to be awesome. You can push the big date back,
run with plan B, or go with what feels light and easy
in the moment. Change is constant; therefore,
resilience is necessary for a happy, stress-free life.
There are times to stand firm, yes, but practice
going with the imperfect flow of life.

. . . .

It wouldn't be called a leap of faith if it was easy,
simple, or something you could predict the outcome of.
Sometimes you simply have to leap. The net will appear,
you'll grow wings, or you may just fall on your face.
Regardless, when your intuition says leap, whatever
the outcome, it's exactly what you need in
this moment. So leap.

344

. . . .

It's not always your responsibility to have the answer, fix things, or make people feel better. It's okay to not know. It's okay to let the responsibility of finding out land on someone else for a change. It's okay to let others take care of themselves so that you can take care of you. The world doesn't have to rest on your shoulders.

345

....

Take the time and space to just be alone in silence.
You can take a walk in nature, pray, meditate, or do
absolutely nothing, but give yourself the space to tap into
a deeper, wiser source. It's hard for wisdom, intuitive hits,
inspiration, and divinity to come through with all the
noise and distractions. Be still, be quiet, be receptive.

346

. . . .

Remember that what you see in others is a
reflection of your beliefs about yourself and the world.
People are simply mirrors, and we see what we project
out into the Universe reflected back to us.
When you find yourself triggered by someone, ask
yourself what could be being projected back towards you.
Where do you need to look within?

347

....

Money loves clarity, so take the time to create
a budget, get clear on where your debt stands,
and paint a clear picture of what you both need
and desire to make financially. The clearer you are
on what you need and where your money goes,
the sooner you can eliminate debt, save up for
that dream trip, or begin making a higher income.

348

. . . .

Stepping into your truth is one of the most challenging, trying, soul-stretching things you'll ever do, but it's so worth it in the end. Every time you speak and act on your truth, you move even more into alignment with your purpose. Your purpose is to be you, and you can't reach it until you start owning your truths.

349

....

Do something just for fun. Something random, silly, unproductive, and maybe even a little childish. Play in a pile of leaves, break out the paints, color in a coloring book while watching reruns of your favorite show. Step away from the day-to-day and give your mind time to relax, explore, and do something new. It will serve your to-do list, I promise.

350

. . . .

If you're not honoring your needs as an individual, those things that make you feel healthy and happy, you're not honoring your relationships, work, family, and friends either. The best thing you can do for them is to show up fully and completely, and that means taking the necessary time for you first and foremost.

351

....

You can be kind, compassionate, supportive,
and understanding and still set firm boundaries.
Being kind doesn't mean allowing people to walk all
over you, take advantage of your time, or be disrespectful
of your needs. Simply express your boundaries clearly,
but with understanding and compassion, then stand firm.

352

. . . .

When you open yourself up to the possibilities within
every situation, especially the challenging ones, you'll find
that there is always something there for you: a lesson,
gift, connection, or experience, exactly what you need to
take your life, career, or happiness to the next level. You'll
only find it if you allow yourself the space of possibility.

353

. . . .

Be a person of integrity, someone who sticks to their word. If you said you'd do something, follow through, even if no one else will know. You will know, and if you don't hold yourself to a higher standard, there's a good chance no one else will. You have to make the choice to be a good, kind, honest person, every day and in every situation.

354

....

Every single day, take one step forward into the unknown
and uncomfortable. Fear and discomfort will always be
there, but it doesn't have to be debilitating. Ease into it,
one micro move at a time. Speak your truth, wear what
you want, stand up tall when you'd normally shy away.
Don't discount the small actions; they add up quickly.

355

. . . .

People are generally good and kind. The ones whose actions or words make them seem otherwise are the ones who need extra love and compassion. Don't resort to negativity just because someone attacks you. Send them light and love. Be kinder than is necessary. Then set stronger boundaries to honor yourself.

356

. . . .

Sometimes you just know something, even if you
don't really know. You know it's time to leave a job,
end a relationship, start your business, or have a baby.
There's no logical surface reason to point to;
you just know. You have to trust this knowing with
all of your being. It's your internal guidance
and it will never lead you astray.

. . . .

If you want to make progress in your life or business,
you have to have a clear end goal in sight. This isn't
about big fancy goals; this is about clarifying your desire.
What do you want to feel, experience, or become?
What is the essence of the goal? Knowing the desire
will help you make solid choices along the way.

358

. . . .

Rewiring yourself is really very simple:
push through the resistance, stay in the present
moment, and get comfortable with the uncomfortable.
That said, simple doesn't mean easy. It takes constant
conscious effort to rewire limiting beliefs, fears, habits,
and blocks. So be kind to yourself and keep on
moving forward; you'll get there.

359

....

Relationships are an energetic exchange, so be respectful
and always honor that. Even if someone is no longer in
your life, either because you chose to release them or they
chose to leave, try to continue respecting that connection.
Honor the relationship through your actions and words.
Stay positive, be kind, and never purposefully cause pain.

360

....

It's okay to slow down, even if there's a lot you have to do. In fact, it's essential to slow down, rest, recover, refill the well, and regain your energy consistently as you work towards achieving goals. The downtime of burnout can be far longer than those few moments, hours, or days you take to do what you need to do to feel awesome.

361

....

Just when you think you have everything under
control and cruising along, something will change.
That's just life. Life is ever changing, as are you and
those you have relationships with. If you're not changing,
you're not growing. So even if the changes are painful,
hard, or poorly timed, be grateful for the
growth you're experiencing.

362

. . . .

Shutting down and shutting people out because they hurt you doesn't fix anything. In fact, it makes things worse. You have to speak up when someone wrongs you, when your feelings are hurt, or you don't like what's being said. The only way to build lasting, fulfilling relationships is to speak your truth, always.

363

....

Just because you can't do something right now doesn't mean you'll never be able to accomplish what you want. Sometimes massive changes take several false starts before you're finally ready to make it happen. Don't let a false start deter you. You learned, you grew, you refocused. Keep trying and you'll get there.

364

....

Sometimes all you can do in a situation is speak your truth. Share your feelings, what's coming up for you, what you need or desire, and what's not working. You don't have to know what it means for the situation; you simply have to show up fully and honestly. The rest will sort itself out naturally.

365

. . . .

We think fear means our intuition is saying,
"No, don't do it!" but really it's the opposite.
Fear means, "Buckle up, it's time to grow and expand!"
Let fear become your guide in life. Whatever you want
to create or accomplish, fear will show up at exactly
the time you need to be nudged forward. Don't let
it deter you from moving forward!

MY *Awesome Life*
MASTERY™

Build a Passion-Based Life and Business™

This year long mastery group gives you complete access to all my products and programs, monthly group coaching calls, a tribe of like-minded people on the same journey as you, and *everything* you need to build a life and business you love! *All for an incredible price.*

....

Use the code ALTBOOK at checkout and save 25%!
www.MyAwesomeLifeMastery.com

....

"People around me have noticed how happy I've been lately and I can 100% say that I have never felt more happy, authentic, confident, and healthy as I do now. I am so grateful to Stephenie for helping me begin this journey of self discovery."

"Hands down, working with [Stephenie] has been one of the best decisions I have ever made."

About the Author

....

Stephenie Zamora is the founder of Stephenie Zamora Media, a full-service, life-purpose development, branding, and online marketing boutique. Here she merges the worlds of personal development, branding, and online marketing to help men and women build passion-based lives and businesses. Stephenie created her business with a simple philosophy: Individuals who take personal responsibility for creating the lives (and jobs) they desire are happier and healthier, and have a greater impact, than those who don't. She is the author of *Awesome Life Tips*™ and creator of My Awesome Life Mastery™. Her articles have been featured in The Huffington Post, Yahoo Shine, Positively Positive, and Brian Tracy International. Learn more about Stephenie at www.StephenieZamora.com!

61142517R00212

Made in the USA
Middletown, DE
07 January 2018